SAGE was founded in 1965 by Sara Miller McCune to support the dissemination of usable knowledge by publishing innovative and high-quality research and teaching content. Today, we publish over 900 journals, including those of more than 400 learned societies, more than 800 new books per year, and a growing range of library products including archives, data, case studies, reports, and video. SAGE remains majority-owned by our founder, and after Sara's lifetime will become owned by a charitable trust that secures our continued independence.

Los Angeles | London | New Delhi | Singapore | Washington DC | Melbourne

ADVANCE PRAISE

Arthur holds our hand along this path of 'Fifty Reflections', but it is much more than that. Reflections at the outset—in the end, during and in between, and throughout the whole book—are all shape shifters, and such is our life, uncatchable, eluding every attempt to organize it. Arthur not only writes words, he evokes emotions that stimulate thinking. And he embraces that trust in life going well beyond thoughts, emotions and words. He provokes us to delve into our existence, it is up to us to attribute a meaning to it and to live by it. Which means feeling worthy of our thoughts and our feelings, welcoming and experiencing them and allowing them to thrive within us.

Arthur leaves us with a special invitation: to understand, notwithstanding our mortal limits, that 'we can cherish ourselves and continue to travel in beauty.' Not that we must, what he means is that we can.

Roberta Sala, *Professor of Political Philosophy, Public Ethics and Bioethics, Università Vita-Salute San Raffaele, Italy*

I have been awaiting Arthur's book, and at last it showed up in my bookcase. It is a book that instils energy, compassion and love, and stimulates us to express our very best. I recommend reading it in peace and quiet and in small doses.

Like sipping a glass of good wine.

Valeria Pruzzi, *Freelance Facilitator for Non-Violent Communication and Partner at Personnel Organization, Italy*

In a frantic world where time flies, this book allows us to stop the ticking of the clock and look within ourselves, listen to our thoughts, observe what is happening and be more aware, so that we can live each day more fully.

Thank you for having distilled life's experiences in deep and practical reflections that manage to speak to the ears of each one of us. A book to keep in your personal library or, even better, in your handbag for whenever you feel like having a moment all for yourself.

Alessandro Cireddu, *After Sales Manager,*
Peroni Pompe SPA, Italy

This book confirms Arthur Sackrule as inspiring a writer as he is a coach, presenter and trainer. It carries universal wisdom and practical considerations, and is nice and easy to read and built upon the insights of brilliant minds. I highly recommend it for every business leader, to learn about how to deal with the dilemmas and the complex issues of these challenging times. A good read that encourages deeper insights and self-reflection. Arthur has done an amazing job of condensing so much information and bringing it to light with a spark.

Aart Pijl, CEO Coach, *Change Company, Netherlands*

These are precious reflections and practices that Arthur Sackrule has produced in his over 30 years of experience and put together in this publication. The book is a real treasure trove of wisdom from which one can tap in daily to discover, rediscover or look for a sense in what we do both inside and outside organizational contexts.

Pasquale Cicchella, *Selection,*
Training and Development Manager,
Air Liquide Healthcare, Italy

[The] book offers 50 marvellous stepping stones for living life—with all its unresolved mysteries—with 'greater completeness and fullness', inviting us to dance from one stone to the other in no particular order. And his offer is made with such elegant simplicity even as it draws on complex research in neuroscience and linguistics. For those of us working on ourselves and working with others as they work on themselves (whether in a personal or professional context), this book brightens the pathways to self-growth. I only wish to add one more stone: read this book. And then dance 'pon the other stones in your living.

Dr Everold Hosein, *Distinguished Scholar,*
City University of New York, School of
Public Health; Senior Communication Advisor,
WHO, Geneva

I met Arthur in 1996, 24 years ago, and from the very start, I knew he was no ordinary person. Never afraid to challenge mediocrity and mainstream lines of thinking, Arthur, throughout all these years has represented a refreshing source of inspiration for my personal and professional development, a long and arduous journey that I know has no end.

After 24 years of walking, seeking and reflecting, I realize now what I've traversed: my personal coast to coast trip, from hell to purgatory and, maybe, now approaching paradise. The stars will be there to tell me whether or not I am on the right track; or in the words of this book as quoted in the next line, I learned the importance of giving and accepting professional feedback which is indeed an art: ' *...when it comes to human interactions, and feedback is offered by a living person ... that is where problems [may] arise.*' Thank you Arthur for being my companion in my personal *Divine Comedy.*

Alberto Nobis, *CEO, DHL Express, Europe*

GRACEFUL
LIVING

GRACEFUL LIVING

50

Reflections for a
Harmonious Life

Arthur A. Sackrule

Los Angeles | London | New Delhi
Singapore | Washington DC | Melbourne

First published in 2021 by

SAGE Publications India Pvt Ltd
B1/I-1 Mohan Cooperative Industrial Area
Mathura Road, New Delhi 110 044, India
www.sagepub.in

SAGE Publications Inc
2455 Teller Road
Thousand Oaks, California 91320, USA

SAGE Publications Ltd
1 Oliver's Yard, 55 City Road
London EC1Y 1SP, United Kingdom

SAGE Publications Asia-Pacific Pte Ltd
18 Cross Street #10-10/11/12
China Square Central
Singapore 048423

Published by Vivek Mehra for SAGE Publications India Pvt Ltd. Typeset in 11.5/14.5pt Bembo by Fidus Design Pvt Ltd, Chandigarh.

Library of Congress Control Number: 2020950877

ISBN: 978-93-5388-728-5 (PB)

SAGE Team: Namarita Kathait, Shipra Pant, Shivani A. Damle and Anupama Krishnan

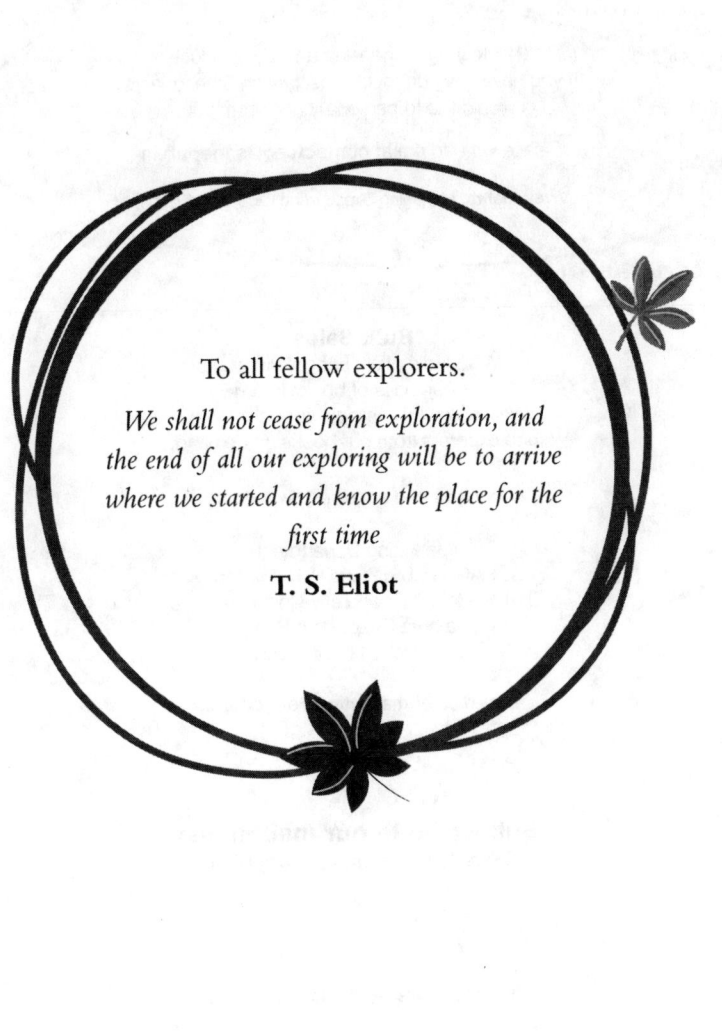

To all fellow explorers.

*We shall not cease from exploration, and
the end of all our exploring will be to arrive
where we started and know the place for the
first time*

T. S. Eliot

Thank you for choosing a SAGE product!
If you have any comment, observation or feedback,
I would like to personally hear from you.

Please write to me at **contactceo@sagepub.in**

Vivek Mehra, Managing Director and CEO, SAGE India.

CONTENTS

FOREWORD

It is a great pleasure to compose this foreword for a book that I myself wanted to write. The field of neurolinguistics has expanded and enriched tremendously through the 40-plus years that I have had the honour to be involved.

Arthur's book feels much like a continuation of this process, which I feel will open the field even more. It feels like a full description which can interact with the other generations of neurolinguistic programming (NLP) and support advancements and enrichments at many levels. I believe it will open up the field even more to the areas of awareness and mindfulness. It makes us aware more fully of our amazing inner landscape and the beautiful relationship of the inner landscape with our human structure and the challenges that the structure by design and by learning inflict upon us. Life is a lot about learning to respond to the challenges that it brings and how to transform them, and it is about the exploration of the edges of our inner world and our perceptions that connect to the beauty of the outer world.

Buddha talked about the veils of misconception, the smoke screens that cause us and others to suffer.

I like to think of these challenges or veils as tyrants. The perceptual ones, where we see the stick many times and that one time we think it is a snake, it's a good thing, as it is related to survival. What is exciting, though, is how our brain is able to take a light wave or a sound wave and translate them into a sound or an image. It is quite a miracle. That wave we cannot see or hear becomes something else because of us. So, we live with the limitation and the miracle at the same time. This is the journey of learning.

Another tyrant is internal dialogue. Maybe those thoughts that get generated through words take us to a degenerative space and place which pulls us away from the beauty of the world and life to an inner space of suffering. Which would we prefer?

Yet another is limited vision or foveal vision. Can I see a world of possibilities or am I limited to a tight laser focus which excludes much of the world? Some say that we got kicked out of the garden of Eden because of short-term, all task, non-relational objectives.

Finally, the tyrant of binary thinking, another possible reason to be kicked out of the garden is the knowledge of good and evil. The good one and the bad one, the good plant and bad plant, for example. It is the classic dilemma, 'Should I do this or that? Which is right or correct or true?' In reality, they are both true and it is with this knowledge that we can become bigger and embrace both truth and also the deeper possible truth.

I express my deepest gratitude to Arthur for this tapestry of many threads that bring so much beauty to us all. My deep thanks to Arthur for including inspirations from the poets, philosophers and storytellers, who have supported this same human endeavour—the endeavour to understand ourselves and how we learn and live.

May you continue to walk in beauty my dear friend and colleague, and thank you for the intelligence and fun you bring to this offering.

—*Judith DeLozier*
Co-developer of neurolinguistic programming,
Santa Cruz

 **PREFACE**

My friend Heinrich Zimmer of years ago used to say, 'The best things can't be told,' because they transcend thought. 'The second best are misunderstood,' because those are the thoughts that are supposed to refer to that which can't be thought about, and one gets stuck in the thoughts. 'The third best are what we talk about.'

—*Joseph Campbell*

This book concerns the third best things and, at the same time, contains reflections and, hopefully, illuminations that will enable us to participate more fully in what the scholar Rudolf Otto called the *mysterium tremedum et fascinans*, which is an eloquent description of what life is about. The book does not aim to be an instruction manual on how to use the brain, rather it is an invitation to travel with joy and confidence through the wonder and the grandeur of this opera of life in which we are participating.

The book is the fruit of extensive research both mine and of the many illustrious people who have accompanied me, in person or through their writings, along the path of my career. Their wisdom that still resonates within me allows me to move forward in harmony, especially in certain difficult moments. A prime example is the incubation of this book, which has lasted several more years than expected.

The book derives from successful practices all over the world, experienced by me in the first person as well as by many other people of different cultures. Consequently, it reflects a sort of universal 'common sense' that can be applied everywhere and anywhere. It conveys the best traditions of wisdom, confirmed by the latest research in neuroscience and made accessible through NLP. The book, which will hopefully be an easy read, does not require any specific knowledge of these two disciplines. The reader will be invited, however, to pause frequently to reflect on its contents.

It is not essential to read the chapters in the order in which they are presented. In addition, some of the contents may deviate from the specific heading of the chapter itself. This will give rise to a more open and freer mode of reflection.

The book does not aim to dispense truths or dogmas. The aim is that its contents can reveal themselves as diamonds of awakening, something that happens to me even up until this day. If some concepts are already familiar, then there is a reason why you are re-reading them. Perhaps they will invite you to a deeper reflection, so that you may put into practice certain principles of life in a more authentic and conscious manner. Or maybe it is to confirm and strengthen them; we all need some reassurance from time to time that we are on the right path. Or again, as in dreams, certain motifs are repeated as a form of healing at an unconscious level.

If you are not in agreement with some of the concepts in the book, I hope that this disaccord may stimulate a constructive and creative dialogue.

It is said that Socrates was sometimes like a horsefly, ready to sting or tease anyone who had become too complacent in their intellectual laziness. I hope you may be appropriately solicited when reading this book, as I was, during its writing.

Finally, it should be remembered that no one becomes a competent sportsman only by reading a book; indeed, reading alone will not replace a training path. An experiential journey assures that learning does not remain just a set of notions, but that these will be transferred to the muscle, to the whole body and to the mind. Usually this process cannot be done alone, we need the support of a guide, a teacher, a mentor or a coach.

According to a Mexican shamanic tradition, made accessible through the writings of Carlos Castaneda, when a person seemed ready to receive the teachings of the shaman Don Juan, they would go to a specific bus stop and only if their intention was genuine, if there really was the desire to learn, the bus would stop and take the person to meet the master. Otherwise, they might have to wait there for years before a bus would stop. When the student is ready, it is said, the master arrives.

I hope this book may open doors behind which masters await you, willing to illuminate a way towards those things that usually cannot be told. A way that allows us to live fully and appreciate the mystery of which we are a part, a mystery that is repeated with every sunrise.

ACKNOWLEDGEMENTS

This section, though a formal requirement of any book, for me is an expression of gratitude towards a universe that, all told, continues to reveal itself as a friendly place.

I wish to thank those masters, too numerous to mention, who with immense generosity, allowed me to participate in their visions and in their dreams. Two in particular stand out. First is Mario Rinvolucri, a pioneer of humanistic-affective teaching in the field of English as a second language, a subject with which I was dealing several decades ago. I met Mario in 1986 and I was struck by his capacity to see and sponsor the potential in others. It was Mario who directed me towards some of the greatest living masters of that period. Every time I met him in the following years, he would enquire about the state of the art of the book I was supposed to be writing. It was a kind of indirect encouragement from this great master. The second, in chronological order, is Judith DeLozier—co-developer of NLP, whom I had met in 1991 in Bali, and I was immediately fascinated by the joy with which she lived her profession, almost like as if she had managed, according to William Blake, to hold the infinite in the palm of her hands. Seeing Judy at work was like magic; she seemed to be able to make words and thoughts dance. This allowed me not only to make the concepts she was teaching my own, but above all to appreciate their beauty.

I wish also to thank the team of Educational Services, the company I created in 1986, whose players today are part of the family unit. They are Lucia—untiring companion, wife and supporter for 50 years now, the person with whom I have shared the significant passages of life together; Alex—son to us, brought up in tradition according to Maria Montessori, a model who through Alex's experience, jump-started my profound process of change that has not yet ended; and Elena—the last entry as a daughter-in-law, who besides being the one who gives me a hand when I want to put into Italian what I think and write, contributed significantly to the language of the original version, Italian, of this book. She is always open to be enchanted and her desire to delve into a mystery is a constant reminder for us all to pursue relentlessly in this direction.

Still, in the family environment, I am grateful to the first person who accompanied me into the mystery of life. I discovered only after she was gone that she was a mother of great love, a person who believed in a universe of harmony and in the inclusion of diversity, concepts that were not necessarily easy to embrace and implement immediately after the Second World War.

Needless to say, this book could not have been published without the generous support of an editor, in this case SAGE Publications. My special thanks goes to the entire SAGE team for their vision and care in enabling this opus to see the light.

I have endeavoured to thank all those on whose shoulders I have been privileged to stand. If you, reader, find something in this book which I have not acknowledged, it is because I am not claiming sole rights. What is now mine has been acquired through exposition in multiple contexts, some of which are now difficult, if not impossible, to trace. What is mine is the fruit of my interaction with others, and sometimes the boundary between mine and that of others becomes blurred. I ask forgiveness for any blatant omissions.

Finally, a special thanks to all clients, and also non-clients, the people with whom I have interacted and who have allowed me to understand something more about the complexity of life by allowing me to enter, I hope respectfully, into their labyrinths.

Thanks in advance to you dear reader, even though I may not know you, because only you can give life to this book. Thanks for the moments that you will want to share through these reflections for life, hoping they can animate your every day, and wishing that you will be a vehicle for their diffusion and, above all will wish to pass them on to future generations.

PERCEPTION

We perceive the world not as it is but as we are.

Why, we ask ourselves, is that person we are talking to are unable to understand our point of view, and why does it take them so long to accept it? We have known each other for ages or at least we thought we did, and so, we are surprised when their ways of thinking are in contrast with ours, with what we deem to be right. Why does this enormous diversity exist beneath the surface, a diversity that sometimes threatens the peaceful coexistence among human beings?

An answer had already been advanced more than two thousand years ago by the philosopher Plato in his allegory of the cave. In this confined space, a group of people have been in chains since their childhood and are forced to face a wall. Behind them is a road and behind it is a fire. When someone passes along the road, their shadow is projected onto the wall and the prisoners, being forced to experience a limited reality, think they see a real person passing in front of them. A similar allegory, found in India, speaks of several blind people around an elephant. Each touches the part closest to them and describes it with a name, for example, a trumpet, a string, a fan and so on. No one is able to see the animal in its entirety and each is convinced that what they are seeing is the right thing.

More recently, in his famous work *Science and Sanity*, 1931, the Polish philosopher-scientist Alfred Korzybski, inspired by the mathematician Eric Bell who said that the map is not the thing that is mapped, coined the famous phrase 'the map is not the territory.' What does this mean? The territory refers to the world and its external stimuli that reaches our five senses. The territory is, therefore, a reality that could be common to all. It is a reality made up of a huge amount of information, calculated to be about 11 million bits per second. Such a gigantic number must be filtered if we are to make sense of anything around us. This process is called mapping and is specific for each individual. In other words, we elaborate the information, each in our own specific way, focusing on some aspects and neglecting others, thus arriving at our own specific mental map based on which we act or react. We can, therefore, speak of an external reality which is common to all and an internal, personal one, which may not be just a passive reaction to sensory inputs, as in the allegories quoted above, but which are actively formed, albeit unconsciously, and which are probably singular to each of us.

The map is, therefore, a unique way in which we perceive and describe what happens around us. It is the sense that we attribute to the events that happen in the territory. The map can, therefore, be defined as the very personal relationship between the observer and the observed. The map is not completely different from the territory; indeed it preserves some of its characteristics and this makes it possible for us to communicate with others. Things get complicated when the map does not refer simply to the description of objects but to states of mind and to the conclusions that are derived from them.

Examining the visual system, whose regions occupy about 35 per cent of the volume of the brain, we find some interesting things. First of all, when we see something, there is not, as was presented in old textbooks, an upside-down image projected at the back of the eye but an intricate network of impulses that travel between the brain and the eye. The brain decides when it has had enough information that will enable it to reach certain conclusions. The exact way in which this happens is still unknown. We do know, however, that this process can sometimes save our skins, for example, when we perceive something that we consider to be a danger but don't wait to process all the information exhaustively to determine if the danger is real or only perceived. Sometimes, it can lead us to conclusions that are too hasty; for example, if we notice that one of our interlocutors is not directly facing us, we may be led to believe that they are not interested in us, and this may compromise the communication.

What we call perception, according to the well-known neuroscientist V. S. Ramachandran in his book *The Tell-Tale Brain*, 2011, is just a hallucination that comes closest to the input of the moment. When our hallucinations have points in common with those of other people, without necessarily coinciding completely, we can speak of being in agreement of having the same point of view.

It all becomes even more complicated when we consider that only a small part of the eye—the fovea, the central part about a millimetre in diameter, focuses and sees in colour. Images arrive at the remaining parts of the eye in a blurry and monochromatic way. What we see, therefore, is largely out of focus, and it is the brain that works wonders to create a sharp and focused image. It could be said that the eye's task is to observe and receive data from the world, while seeing and perceiving is the brain's task.

And it doesn't end there. The eye does not just look at the point we are interested in focusing on, but with fast and jerky movements called saccades, which occur at a frequency of about three–four times a second, it scans, without any head movements, a larger area of which we are not even aware. In addition, blinking makes our vision intermittent, so much so that it is calculated that the visual system is offline, inactive for about four hours during our waking day. Despite all this, we are able to find continuity in what we are looking at. We can understand why it is said that perception is a great illusion and, sometimes, a great disappointment.

These physiological factors, according to the recent calculations, account for about 10 per cent of our differences in perception, while 90 per cent is due to personal factors. Perception, being a relationship between the observer and the observed, depends largely on certain inherent factors, for example, our temperament, our idiosyncrasies and the emotional state in which we find ourselves. It seems that only those aspects that we believe to be emotionally meaningful will capture our attention. The others are more or less neglected. Given that there are over seven billion inhabitants on earth, we may conclude that there are as many ways of perceiving, that is, of understanding reality. Finding ourselves in agreement on the perception of an event or a phenomenon can truly be considered a miracle.

The way we remember past events and how we anticipate the future contribute to form our personal map. The outcome of pleasant or unpleasant encounters, the experience of examinations passed or failed, and other similar factors inevitably leave a trace, a mandatory road that largely determines our future elaborations. The glass will, therefore, be perceived as half full or half empty, and this describes our map of reality, familiar and unchangingly rigid. Not only does it direct our perception, but it becomes a sort of funnel that conditions the way we approach the future, for example, with courage, distrust or anything else.

We can talk about sticky maps which we carry with us at all times. These are maps that make us reason in such a way as to confirm what we were elaborating. If, for example, we were robbed while we were in the car and we came to the conclusion that the roads are unsafe, it is likely that the mere fact that someone approaches us while we are at a traffic light will confirm this and at the same time strengthen our conviction. If we perceive the world as a hostile place, even arriving late to catch a train, which obviously has already left the station, may well confirm our hypothesis that the world is indeed against us.

A very interesting consideration is that, thanks to our perceptual filters and based on our own limited interpretations, we draw conclusions that, in fact, decide how we will deal with the next moments of life, with optimism or with pessimism, for example. We can, therefore, say that by means of our perception, we are, at all times, helping to shape our future.

Our rigid maps, although different from other rigid maps, can be a significant source of conflicts, even degenerating into wars as is often seen in matters of religion and politics. Even our day-to-day decisions, for example, how to raise children or how to manage employees can cause considerable disagreements. We each defend our position, trying to overrule those of others to show that our opinion is right while that of the others is wrong.

Keeping in mind the mantra that the map is not the territory but it is only the relationship between the observer and the observed will go towards making us more understanding in our interpersonal relationships. We will certainly violate this principle again but reviewing a conversation that didn't go as well as we wanted, we can identify different moments in which we became terribly attached to our own mental map. By so reflecting, we may be able to understand our interlocutor's map more fully.

Such a systematic way of taking distance and reviewing what we have done is a highly effective training, because it will allow us to become a little faster in recognizing and appreciating that everyone is elaborating reality according to their own individual patterns. Our maps will consequently become less rigid, more open and wider. And we will be more ready to welcome diversity the next time we come across a map that is completely different from ours.

Appreciating such diversity is yet another important step towards wisdom.

HIJACKED BY OUR BRAIN

A wild untrained mind can keep us trapped in some very uncomfortable places.

—*Pema Chodron*

Imagine we are walking along a path, perhaps in a forest, and chance to see a stick. In a flash, we think we saw a snake and we begin to have some of the typical reactions for such a situation—fear, acceleration of breathing and heart rate, and increased sweating. The person we were walking with saw something different and assures us or tries to reassure us that it was just a stick. But it is too late, our brain has already deceived us and the illusion has turned into fear. We are at a loss for what to do, we may feel stuck, frozen or we may run for our lives. On some occasions, but only if we really feel up to it, we may contemplate launching an attack on the imaginary snake.

Such things happen in a fraction of second, thanks to the speed with which our brain takes care of us. It is a question of survival as it is better to mistake a stick for a snake than a snake for a stick. The speed with which these elaborations occur depends largely on our system of perception, which stops processing once it believes it has had sufficient information to decide. Our brain will continue offering us choices that have become consolidated, some inherited from our reptilian ancestors in the distant past. These are choices that may be defined as rigid which unfortunately does not allow any new information to arrive, for example, to imagine how the stick would look if it were resting on an asphalted road.

An analogy could be drawn between these situations and those in which we find ourselves completing someone's sentence, putting words into their mouth as such. The tendency to arrive at hasty conclusions based on fragments of information is often, as we have seen, a question of survival. This means we are acting as predators, trying to dominate, or to avoid becoming prey, in any case, trying to escape from danger. We may ask ourselves if by completing the phrase of another, we are using the same mechanism of domination.

Returning to the case of the stick–snake, the decision-making process, which in these circumstances allows us to reach certain conclusions, may be attributed largely to the amygdala—that part of the brain that looks like a small almond and is responsible for our emotional reactions, especially negative ones. In humans, under normal conditions, there is a collaboration between the amygdala and the frontal cortex, the part that handles reasoning. Sometimes, however, this collaboration is interrupted and our conclusions are no longer mediated by the use of reason and common sense but are dominated by the amygdala. It is as if this part has taken over, technically speaking, hijacking the working of our brain. This inhibits any collaboration with the frontal cortex, the part of our brain which could have informed us that it was only a stick we had seen and that there was nothing to worry about. In such situations, we may say that the person has gone out of their mind.

According to some scholarly research, our brain recognizes two and only two fundamental states; one is the threat to our survival with consequent fear and increased adrenaline, and the other is gratification and satisfaction from the release of dopamine. Inherited from the animal kingdom from which it is assumed that we derive, the amygdala together with other structures in the limbic system—that is, the emotional brain—works, also based on our past experiences, to determine if what we encounter is friendly or hostile. This is an extremely rapid process that takes place in the space of about 15 milliseconds, compared to the 100 milliseconds that reasoning would take. In the limbic brain, there are 6 billion nerve cells firing each second, compared to the few 100 stimulations in the frontal cortex—the rational, logical part of the brain.

This is what happens even in less extreme but very frequent circumstances, for example, when it comes to certain topics such as football, politics and geopolitics, where there could be contrasting points of view. Other examples can be ways of doing things, such as how a person rattles the coins in their pocket, how they drink or chew, attitudes that, for some strange reason, are able to trigger a strong reaction in an observer. Without realizing it, we may experience these differences as a threat to our status quo. We feel not only that we must defend our map, but that ours is the right one while all others are wrong. We may even consider the situation as a threat, in which case, the amygdala has again taken centre stage. It can be said that we have been hijacked by the emotional part of our brain.

What to do in such situations? It is obvious that attempting to reason with someone who has been captured or seized by the amygdala, trying to minimize their discomfort, saying, for example, that everything will be all right will have very little effect. Their brain is still in survival mode, that is, fight, flight or remaining frozen in the hope that the perceived danger will cease. Nature has not provided us with the ability to reflect in this situation but only to safeguard ourselves. Only after a while, when the situation ultimately returns to normal can we afford the use of reason. If we want to be supportive to those who are suffering, we can offer a few words of comfort, thereby making our presence felt without necessarily trying to resolve the situation. We can allow the other person to appreciate be aware that we understand their situation and maybe radiate love in the manner most appropriate to the circumstance. We can simply radiate the thought that no sentient being needs to suffer excessively.

We can, however, train the brain to deal with these situations knowing that, thanks to its plasticity, it has the ability to change not only at a young age, but at all stages of life. We can, therefore, change our usual emotional reactions by devoting a little attention to them. We can take note of the words, gestures and tones of voice that derail us and decide what to do to avoid being hijacked. Some simple steps could be to distract ourselves as soon as the symptoms are noticed, perhaps by directing our attention elsewhere, thus, allowing the brain to regain its proper functioning. If we have an object at hand, for example, a key ring, we could hold it and play with it. Even a phone call to someone can serve to restore balance in the brain.

It would also be useful to realize how our breath has changed in these moments of tension. But even more useful would be to train ourselves to breathe with our diaphragm. To put it simply, this means letting the belly area, not the chest, expand during the inhalation phase and allowing it to contract during the exhalation phase. It is important not to impose a particularly slow pace for the breath but simply to support the ongoing breath, giving attention to the movement in the belly area. Calming the breath this way serves to create more space within us. The impact of strong emotions diminishes, their effect being like that of a pinch of salt thrown into a lake rather than into a glass of water. We will be freer to generate alternative behaviours.

Another useful thing to know is that if a person is being a prey to emotions, as can be seen by changes in their voice tone, face colour and breath, it is very likely that their system is ready to fight or flee. In each case, there is an increase in adrenaline, their muscles are ready to act and there is a greater release of glucose in the blood. A short fast walk or a run would serve to consume the glucose and to relax the muscles, assisting our system to return to a more balanced state.

The latest neuroscience research confirms that when we are in a state of emotional safety, we are in a sort of safe haven and we are more able to manage surprises. We are more open to new ideas, less dogmatic and more ready to manage ambiguity. This is the condition in which we find ourselves naturally when someone who is particularly dear holds our hand, giving us a sense of reassurance, the sense of 'being in good hands'. If we don't have someone physically present who can give us this kind of comfort, we can also create it by remembering and reliving a couple of situations in which we were at ease, possibly in an empathic and intimate relationship with someone who loves us. Our brain will be able to offer us similar sensations even if they are only being relived.

We can really equip our brain to prevent and to deal with adversity, a condition that always seems to be lurking in life. A life, according to Emily Dickinson, that is so startling it leaves little time for anything else.

THE TIP OF
THE ICEBERG

*If the doors of perception were cleansed, everything would appear to man
as it is, infinite.*

—*William Blake*

The distinction between map and territory is a really useful model that enables us to understand how we attribute meaning to the universe. The information that comes to us from the world, that is, from the territory and that could be the same for everyone, undergoes changes according to our own personal configuration, for example, our state of mind, our past and our expectations for the future. We could talk about a new territory that is formed, an internalized territory, our own elaboration of reality. In this process, we communicate its results first to ourselves and then to others. During the act of communication, both regarding ourselves and others, a further transformation can be seen. We use other filters, the sum of which gives rise to our own mental map—our unique experience of reality. This contributes to differentiate one individual from another.

To understand better how this transformation takes place, what Noam Chomsky calls transformational grammar, we can consider a detailed map of a city which includes its streets, the main places of interest, urban transport routes and subway lines. The wealth of information is such that, for example, the one who is only interested in subway stops would have great difficulty detecting them at first glance. A map that is so detailed would only be a hindrance. In the same vein, the information that comes to us from the world is so much, reckoned to be about 11 million pieces of information per second, that we must act on it to make it more manageable.

The three filters that human beings apply universally for this purpose are deletion, generalization and deformation or distortion. These describe how we all create our own reality, our individual map. The advantage of having a well-defined map saves us from having to continually re-elaborate the data coming from the territory, while on the other hand, it limits us because we risk drawing too hasty conclusions. We can, therefore, say that the way we express ourselves is merely a fraction of our entire being, the tip of the iceberg.

DELETION

In this mechanism, certain aspects of the incoming information are ignored in order to give more attention to others. This allows us to resize and reduce it so as not to be overwhelmed by its overabundance. Without a good process of deletion, we will not be able to translate our thoughts into words.

In our daily life, we are bombarded by a myriad of stimuli, most of which we ignore. If we just stopped for a moment, we may become aware of how many noises are around us which we were not aware of before such as the traffic, an overhead plane, the chirping of birds, the hum of the computer, the engine of the air conditioner and the water in the pipes. The same is true for what arrives in our visual field, how many objects, colours and shapes there are that if we stopped to observe them, we could be so absorbed as to forget what we were doing before. In the analogy of the city map, we must erase all that could distract us from the path to our destination.

This is a process that already takes place in a young child who, seeing several chairs and in order to be able to say that all are chairs, must erase the superfluous aspects, for example, the colours and the upholstery because these could distract from the essence of the object being observed. This is an important moment for the child's growth—being able to give a name to objects, thereby creating a certain stability in their world which could otherwise remain vague and elusive.

Even as adults, we can see the same phenomenon. Perhaps we come to the conclusion that a certain person is conceited because they move without even offering a passing glance to those around them. We may have deleted several factors in the rush to pigeonhole the person. We may have overlooked the fact that they may be shy or that they may be lacking in self-esteem. We want or need to simplify the complexity of the universe to make it a little more understandable, giving explanations to everything that happens, even ignoring and deleting information that could give a more complete interpretation. This map of ours thus becomes limiting because every future behaviour of the person, even if not really relevant, would go to confirm our opinion. In this way, the map becomes sticky, that is, it becomes the filter through which we elaborate future experiences.

Deletion also takes place for cultural reasons. Man, perhaps because of his past as a hunter, intent on reaching his prey, tends to ignore certain elements of the landscape around that a woman would detect, for example, colours and shapes. Even a frog has its filters, it captures everything that moves, even if not edible, while it will ignore a fly that died recently, in other words—fresh meat, even if it is within its reach.

Deletion is also an important factor in our choices. For example, we may go outdoors even if our body, perhaps feverish, is telling us that it would be better to stay inside, be quiet and have some rest. Or we sacrifice important projects for more futile things.

In these cases, it could be said that certain information falls on our blind spot, that point inside the eye that is devoid of cones and rods and, therefore, unable to process what impacts the eyes.

Deletion may be somewhat similar to repression in the Freudian sense in which unpleasant parts of experiences are suppressed, or akin to denial, according to Kübler-Ross' *On Death and Dying*, 1969, in which the person seems to deny obvious evidence.

GENERALIZATION

The second mechanism—generalization is, in a sense, the opposite of deletion and is equally essential for our learning process. It refers to the ability to extract meaningful parts of an experience and apply and use them in other contexts. This process, which is typical in arithmetic, allows rules to be applied in different contexts. In the same vein, once we have learned to drive on one road, we are able, at least theoretically, to drive on other roads. Again, as we learned to turn on the light in one room, we can generalize and press a similar button or flick a similar switch in another room, confiding that the light will turn on. Another example is that by accepting the generalization that lions are fierce, we do not need to test a future encounter with a lion to verify if it is fierce, we can infer on the basis of past learning, thereby ensuring our safety and survival.

Sometimes, however, differences are neglected, and we end up lumping everything together. In this case, generalization becomes a rigid way of thinking. It is the case of stereotypes, where we may attribute, for example, a certain quality to all men, to all women, or even to an entire population. On a more day-to-day level, if we have had a positive experience with a certain person, the next time we meet up, we will tend to have a similarly positive experience again. The same is clearly true if the first experience was negative. Our human need is to have the fewest number of possible variables in order to maintain a certain stability and certainty, to connect the dots, even inventing connections where they do not exist. If we wake up in our neighbourhood one morning and we see new work in progress, we may immediately be led to hypothesize the reasons behind this. Others, of course, will have different speculations according to their own mental map.

The hurry to reach a conclusion is also seen in the phenomenon of pareidolia, the experience in which a specific form is perceived where it does not actually exist. In the images sent from the planet Mars, especially in the mountainous region of Cydonia, we seem to perceive a human face, which, in reality, does not exist. Our uncertainty is sometimes so destabilizing, like the feeling of walking on fish, that we feel the need to scramble quickly to reach solid ground. Sometimes, it seems that we must reorganize reality to conform to our maps to our own points of view.

In the analogy of the metropolitan map, generalization is a very useful way to proceed. All stations are represented as if they were the same, small dots on the map, ignoring any differences whatsoever that exist between them, thus, facilitating reading the map.

DEFORMATION

Mark Twain in his autobiography said that in his life there had been a lot of tragedy, maybe half of it really happened. This refers to our ability to deform or distort the meaning of our experiences, to make them more in line with our expectations. It is reckoned that if all our memories were precise, life would be rather dull and boring. Memory in this sense is more a poet than a historian.

The ability to deform allows us to inhabit the world of fiction, to create and appreciate stories and to confabulate. When we listen to a story, we are naturally inclined to put ourselves in the shoes of the protagonist, to take on his identity and this develops our capacity for empathy.

Deformation also allows us to delude ourselves, to live in the world of make-believe, as if things have already happened. When we look in the mirror, for example, putting on our make-up and preparing ourselves for an important meeting, or when we try on a new dress in a store, we will probably project ourselves into the future image of how we wish to be perceived. And we convince ourselves, with good reason, that this reality has already happened. This incredible capacity allows children to use role models thereby learning quickly by emulating others.

Other examples of deformation are when we decide that one thing has priority over another we establish arbitrary scales according to our mental map. In addition, the ability to innovate and think out of the box, seeing solutions where there were none before, means putting more emphasis on certain aspects of a situation and distorting them with respect to others.

Some deformations, whose intentions are to speed up our processing from the territory to the map, can be counterproductive. For example, we may happen to misinterpret someone's gaze, due to our mental state in that moment. Even words that are spoken may be taken too personally. We may be convinced that we know the intentions of our interlocutor, again, to hasten reaching conclusions but at the expense of accuracy. When food is left on the plate, for example, someone could intervene not only asking us if we did not like the food but may feel offended, while the matter was simply that our hunger had been appeased. The temptation to imagine being able to read another's thoughts is strong.

A typical aspect of deformation is when a problem is magnified. We may be going up a path in the mountains and the peak seems very far away due to fatigue, while the same peak is a piece of cake when we are more rested. In the same way, we magnify certain daily challenges, sometimes due to our physical state and sometimes due to past experiences. For example, failure in a test could lead to reasoning like, 'Because I failed, it means that I am incapable', with the consequent lowering or loss of self-esteem.

REMEDIES

It seems simple enough to understand that what we think and say to ourselves or to others is only the smallest fraction of the original input, which remains submerged below the surface. In this sense, our thoughts, ideas and words are the result of the processes of transformation, namely deletion, generalization and deformation and, therefore, represent the tip of the iceberg.

Problems arise when the visible part, that is, the tip is mistaken for the truth, the absolute truth, separating it from its underside and transforming it to create our mental map. We end up being rigid, inflexible, limiting our possibilities for growth and change. When we communicate with others, convinced that the tip of the iceberg is the whole truth, we risk creating contrasts that can lead to conflicts, tyrannies and wars.

QUESTIONS

We must avoid stopping at words alone and go beyond their surface meaning. We need to travel into that vast territory below the tip of the iceberg so as to investigate what was deleted, generalized or deformed. And to do this, so as not to be deceived by the weight of words, both with respect to ourselves and others, we can take advantage of the support of questions.

Questions have the power to stimulate thought in a different way. Appropriately formed, they invite us to reverse the process of elaboration thereby recovering more of the original territory before the map was formed, in other words, before the conclusion was reached.

One of the most useful questions offered in an inviting and respectful tone is, 'How do you know that what you are saying is true?' This is a question we can ask not only to others, but also to ourselves, and when appropriately repeated, it invites us to dive down into the processes that gave rise to our thoughts. Professionally done, it could be like descending into the belly of the whale, the place where dogmas and rigid attachments loosen and where we are more closely in touch with the sources of our experience.

Of course, many other questions can be asked. As Einstein said, the important thing is never to give up asking questions.

THE MEANING OF CHANGE

The only constant in life is change

—*Heraclitus*

A very interesting manifestation of change is one that concerns our body. According to the well-known holistic doctor, Deepak Chopra as stated in his book *Ageless Body, Timeless Mind*, 1993, our body renews itself every year by 98per cent. The pancreas regenerates most of its cells every 24 hours, the cells of the stomach lining reproduce themselves every 3 days, our white blood cells every 10 days and 98per cent of the protein in the brain in less than a month. The cells of our skin renew themselves at a speed of one hundred thousand per minute (most of house dust is made of dead cells.) We have a new skin every month and a new liver every six weeks. In a sense, we are no longer the same person as we were a minute before.

Nevertheless, change is sometimes more difficult than it seems. An example of this is what happened in a zoo, where the bear was used to walking along the perimeter of its cage. One day, they decided to make its environment more naturalistic, widening the limits of the enclosure, thus incorporating it somewhat into the surrounding landscape. What did the bear do? It kept walking along the old perimeter for a few months. Even human beings are similar except for the fact that they seem to take much longer than an animal to make the change!

We come across so many examples in our everyday life, for example, sitting at the same place at the dinner table, using the same glass, always putting on the right shoe before the left one and so on. We could say that we are all creatures of habit. Not to mention the less banal gestures, but equally important, for example, lighting up a cigarette after coffee, looking at the smartphone as soon as we get out of the car and keeping looking at it while walking.

These are our so-called comfort zones. Abandoning them costs in terms of effort. Our brain is an organ that consumes a lot of energy when we face our daily challenges, some of which may take us back to the age of the hunter-gatherer, in other words, predator against prey. Just staying healthy, without succumbing to harmful bacteria and viruses is a non-trivial, balancing game. For these reasons, we tend to save energy or effort in any action we perform so as to have a reserve of resources that we can count on for any other dangers that we may encounter.

The need to change is particularly felt today, in a world that has become more and more volatile, uncertain, complex and ambiguous. Some of our old ways of acting are no longer adequate. In the past, it was common to throw rubbish out of the car window while traveling and for some, this is still an automatic gesture. Once it was normal to discharge wastes from production into rivers or into the sea. Similar actions would be unthinkable today, even though some people still persist in doing so. But there are also those little things we do every day. How do we respond to a provocation? Are we still in the world of dinosaurs where the strongest survives? Or in the world of human beings in which flexibility, not strength, is the driving force? In the area of health and with new discoveries in medicine and neuroscience, the exhortation to change is even stronger, especially as far as some lifestyle habits are concerned, for example, smoking and drinking in excess or being too sedentary. We are invited to moderate the use of substances and to practise movement and sport.

Fortunately, our brain is endowed with a quality called neuro-plasticity, that is, the ability to change many of its aspects even at an advanced age. The surprising results of patients afflicted with strokes who manage to recover a large percentage of their functions are testimony to our capacity for change.

But when the change is proposed as doing the opposite of what was done before, our brain, because it is an energy saving device, tends to rebel. Doing the opposite of what we did before often requires us to put a stop to our habitual behaviour, and the brain gets tired in a hurry when it has to act on its brakes. Correcting a child who tells lies by forbidding them from lying or admonishing that they must always tell the truth becomes difficult to sustain for any length of time.

We can facilitate change by taking inspiration from the Greek etymology of the word 'change', which means to turn around, to bend or to curve. This makes the concept of change less challenging, because it is not necessary to do the opposite of what was being done before. So, it is not about throwing away old choices and adopting new ones. It is no longer a binary—black or white reasoning—which is often limiting, but change becomes more of a process of adding choices, choices that allow us to live life at a level of greater completeness and fullness.

To begin with, it is useful to accustom ourselves with the concept of change by introducing some small and simple varia-tions, whose execution does not require a great consumption of energy. We can carry out some exercises of mindfulness, a term which means being more present in what we do and training our awareness accordingly. With a little care, we can identify some habitual actions, for example, how we make the bed, how we bring a glass to our lips, on which foot we put on our socks or shoes first. We can decide to make some small changes to these activities, dedicating a few more seconds of attention. This costs little in terms of energy but has a huge yield. Our brain manages to leave its comfort zone gradually, and the message that is transmitted is that of plasticity, in other words, change is possible. It is even more effective if we create a routine of repeating these little changes at the same time, every day. It is important to note that in all these actions there is no great disruption which could make the brain rebel, there is only an invitation to change something, in this case, by means of greater attention. The brain can go back to doing as it did before, in which case, the comfort zone will not have been cancelled but simply expanded.

These are changes that surely succeed in positively deceiving the brain, making it believe that it has more possibilities than those expressed up until this point. It is a question of widening its possibilities, a bit like putting more chairs and armchairs in a room. Surely, we will have more choices as to where to sit, we will see things from different angles, but we will always be in the same room.

This is transactional change. But change can also be at a transformational level.

Going back to the metaphor of the rooms, what would it be like if we could climb to higher floors? What new points of view will we have? Einstein reminds us that change does not come about through the same kind of thought, that is, at the same level that brought about a situation. In correcting a wrong action, whether of a child or an adult, it is better to explain why instead of just prohibiting or proposing alternatives. The sole fact of proposing—or rather, evoking alternatives, even though it will allow the brain to understand that change is possible—may prove ineffective after diverse repetitions if the alternatives do not lead to an expansion of the way of thinking. Transformational alternatives, on the other hand, starting with explaining why, are the ones that allow us to open doors to new worlds, or as Proust said, to see the same world with new eyes.

What makes change even more challenging is the environment in which a person finds themselves. The one who wants to quit smoking, drinking or being attached to the smartphone, but stays in the company of those who are dependent on these habits, could experience great difficulty to change, when the only alternative is to do the opposite of what was done before.

Transformational change takes reasoning to another level, creating more motivation to find other ways of acting. The alternatives to be implemented not only concern what to do, but how we will feel as a consequence, for example, happier and more peaceful. These new ways of acting can also come from answering questions concerning the type of person we will become, the new possibilities that we will have and the extra developments that we will be able to achieve in our life. These are questions that refer to the area of our desires and dreams, often not made explicit, and serve to guide us towards greater openness through the actions of bending, curving or turning around, all of which facilitate change.

In fact, our responses will enable us to create a different relationship with our habits. If, for example, we tend to sink in an armchair in front of the television after dinner, transformational questions will lead to a new way of engagement after dinner. We can still watch the television, sit in the same chair but relate differently to the moment, for example, using it to recharge ourselves in a conscious manner or to respond responsibly to the stimuli that come from the television, avoiding compulsive zapping. Simply put, we can experience this moment with another spirit.

The great inventor Buckminster Fuller said that the best way to change is to propose a new model that makes the current one obsolete. This may well be the essence of change.

TRAINING AND LEARNING

It can be said that we have learned something when it remains etched in our mind, that is, when we have fast, if not instant, access to the content in question. This can range from the simple memorization of a sentence or a paragraph to the acquisition of new skills for managing aspects of our life. In the early stages of our existence, when we were children, learning was ongoing and it required a great deal of awareness. It was the period when the motto 'you learn something new every day' held true. However, as we grow, our attention becomes more selective, partly due to the environment in which we live and which limits our openness to certain stimuli that, in any case, keep coming from the world. In a classic experiment, it was shown that at the age of seven months, Japanese children had no problem discriminating the sounds of 'r' and 'l' of European languages, while at the age of ten months, they were no longer able to differentiate them. As adults, the situation changes again. Not only have we lost the ability to discriminate, but also to allow new information to enter the brain. It is estimated that of the 50 thousand thoughts we have per day, or according to some sources, 70 thousand, 95 per cent are the same as yesterday.

The situation can be compared to three pots, according to the Buddhist nun Pema Chodron in her book *No Time to Lose*, 2005. The first pot is completely filled with opinions and preconceptions where we think we know everything. This prevents any new content from allowing us to question our ideas. The second pot contains poison and is like a cynical, critical mind, so ready to judge that any new content is contaminated by this rigidity, not granting us the openness necessary to explore something that can challenge the status quo. The third pot is full of holes and it's like a distracted mind, the body is present, but the thoughts are so absorbed elsewhere in some pressing commitment or thinking about an upcoming appointment that anything new escapes us.

Today, there is another phenomenon that aggravates the situation. We are witnessing a constant rush, everything seems like a race against time, everything becomes an emergency, not only in work, but even in something as mundane as eating and this attitude has also become part of the approach towards learning. The expectation is that of immediate results, we often hear of training pills, a kind of instant gratification, almost an intellectual consumerism. In this type of consumerism, the human attention span has fallen to only eight seconds, while that of a goldfish remains nine seconds.

Learning, however, always takes place through pathways in the brain and these are formed by the synaptic connections between neurons. When information arrives, the brain, in order to be able to make use of it, must find, in a fraction of a second, a neuronal connection across the synapses. When this operation is performed automatically, in other words, in real time, it can be said that learning has taken place. Before this happens, however, it is necessary to create a path. This is like walking in a field of tall grass where, after the first crossing, the grass flattens out only to rise up again. Only after repeated walks or by passing with a heavy object—for example, a road roller— would the grass remain crushed for any length of time, thus, creating a new track. This is what happens in the brain as well; after some time and after different repetitions, the automatism is created.

If the new path is no longer used, that is to say if the new information is not used, the path disappears. As the saying goes, 'use it or lose it'. We retain our learning through training. Training means developing a good energy that supports us in facing fatigue with tenacity and enthusiasm, factors that allow us to keep fit or prepare for an important event. Training can take place both in extension and in depth. The first type refers to repetitions; the second, more akin to a road roller, works on the emotional intensity of the experience we are going through. An example of the latter is fears and phobias, whose learning takes place through a single exposure, thanks to the presence of the part of the brain called amygdala.

Returning to the first type, the one based on the number of repetitions, some sources state that it takes about 21 days to notice changes in a habit. Only then are the new choices delegated to the basal ganglia in the brain, the part responsible for automatisms, which allows the brain to operate in its preferred energy saving mode. For change to remain, we must continue to put the new learning into practise. According to research conducted at the Berlin Academy of Music[1] on violinists, those who became a violin teacher had trained for 4 thousand hours over the course of their lives. The good violinists had trained for 8 thousand hours, while the stars for 10 thousand hours. It is known that athletes train continuously, it is estimated that training takes up 95 per cent of their time, while competitions account for the remaining 5 per cent. This is an important message for those who think,

---

[1] Malcom Gladwell, *Outliers: The Story of Success* (New York: Little, Brown and Company, 2011), 35–68.

typically in the workplace, that when it comes to learning something new, learning takes place through only one exposition, for example, a short training course.

However, repetition alone is not enough to lay the pathways to create learning. It needs to be done with awareness. Trying to learn while one runs on the treadmill, usually, does not give good results, neither for the body nor for the mind, because the attention is defocused. It is not, therefore, a question of mechanical repetition but of targeted training, sometimes called smart practice, done with regularity and with the conscious search for continuous improvement, also by means of small expedients. This can be seen in sports where a few grams or a slightly altered aerodynamic shape can make a world of difference. Improving by 1 per cent per day, according to a mathematical calculation, will result in a 100 per cent improvement in 72 days.

Repetitions can also be done virtually. By visualizing, in as much detail as possible, the carrying out of an action that we wish to perform in the future and the final result we want to attain we will activate the same circuits in the brain as if we had done a physical repetition. The effectiveness of visualization can be further increased through embellishment. For example, if we wish to visualize a good performance in a meeting, we could add the enthusiastic faces of other people; if we visualize a meeting with someone who, in the past, was a source of unease, a smile could be added or the image of the sun that illuminates and gives warmth or other similar elements. A good practice is to do these visualizations combining them with other routine activities we do, for example, while brushing our teeth. There are really many possibilities of learning through visualization.

The second way to train, in depth, is to use neuropeptides, that is, the molecules of emotions. These are the substances that the brain uses to create neuronal connections. Learning is, therefore, not only a mechanical question, but has a strong emotional component. It is necessary to provide our training with pleasant emotional stimuli that can support learning. A pleasant climate that creates a positive association, a compassionate teacher, a book written by a well-respected person are all factors that facilitate learning, reducing the need for an enormous expenditure of effort. The context in which one can experiment what one is learning also serves to consolidate learning. A person who is learning a foreign language and would like to start putting it into practise, would be better off starting in a sufficiently protected, holding environment, so as to create a state of calm and confidence that will contain what they will say and the feedback they will receive.

It is useful to remember, however, that the best learning happens when what we learn is close to our hearts and will serve our improvement and growth. Learning something because it is fashionable or because someone else forces us could produce effects that are not really gratifying. 'Don't let the noise of others' opinions drown out your own inner voice,' said Steve Jobs. 'And most important, have the courage to follow your heart and intuition. They somehow already know what you truly want to become. Everything else is secondary.'

A final consideration, which particularly concerns passages or poems that we want to learn is to read them aloud. By doing so, we make use of three parts of our brain reinforcing the learning we wish to obtain. The three parts are the Wernicke area which includes written and spoken language, the area of Broca, that is, related to the production of speech and the temporal lobe that contains the auditory centres of the brain. This is also an explanation why we remember better catchy rhymes and slogans.

6

GENIUS IS BORN OR MADE

If you knew how much work I put into it, you wouldn't call me a genius.

—*Michelangelo Buonarroti*

This is one of those issues that give rise to heated conversations not just in the living room, but also in the world of science and, consequently, around the topic of learning. In the second area, we hear talk about being cut out for a subject, in which case, it is worth devoting time and effort which would otherwise be wasted if the person were not so endowed. We also hear about talented people, often with the connotation of a gift from nature. The discussion can easily escalate to referring to a person's character, something etched in stone that cannot be changed.

There are no definitive answers but one thing we know is that the gene of genius has not yet been discovered. Many advances have, however, been made by neuroscience in recent years. Biographies also present us with some evidence that would indicate the importance of the environment in the development of a person. An example is Mozart—a recognized musical genius. Encouraged to play since childhood, he received a lot of feedback from his family that supported and strengthened him at a tender age. Does this factor determine success?

We can compare the case of Mozart with what happens in most cases when a young child performs, for example, singing in the company of family or friends. If the note sung is not accurate and clean, the parent could feel a little embarrassed, since they do not want to let it be known that their child has made a mistake. Seeing the young one as a reflection of themselves, the parent tries to silence them or to make fun of the situation so as to avoid embarrassment. If instead, the note was clean and precise and the parent recognizes the child's singing ability, the risk is that they will be quickly sent off to a master. If this teacher does not have an approach to learning that will evoke the child's potential, the risk is that of suffocating them in the name of performance, directing them towards a competitive environment in which the intention is to squeeze out every gram of their ability. In such a situation, the nutritional feedback support that Mozart enjoyed will be lacking.

Neuroscience tells us, however, that the space in the brain reserved for the ability of a professional—for example, a musician—is greater than that of someone who does not show such leanings. But what is perhaps most relevant is that when the skill is trained, the space occupied in the brain increases not only during but even after childhood. Studies on brain neuroplasticity[2] in the latter half of the 20th century confirm that the brain does not have a static configuration, an inherited one, but it can be modified and trained according to one's will and also according to the mental states that a person experiences. Indeed, the quality and the amount of care, attention and affection that a child receives influences their behaviour and growth. As a result, some genes may remain silent while others may be very active. And it is often the interaction with the environment that activates them. Studies on adopted children placed in contexts full of stimuli and relationships with significant people seem to confirm how important interaction is, even in adulthood. Many aspects of our body and our behaviours appear to be the result of

---

[2] https://www.ncbi.nlm.nih.gov/pmc/articles/PMC3222570/

complex interactions between genes and the environment, even though some combinations are random.

The discussion whether genius is born or made, sometimes, serves to inhibit the possibilities of change through proclamations of the kind that one is born in a certain way, everything is preordained, or if something is destined to happen, it will happen. These are all thoughts that threaten to undermine our efforts and in the long run, our existence. The extreme conclusion is that things cannot be changed, in contrast to the recent discoveries on neurogenesis—the ability in some parts of the brain to generate new neurons at any age. This argument becomes a sort of alibi for laziness or for not having managed to make changes, and it is also a way of condemning others who failed to change, with the hope that by condemning someone else, we are safe from criticism.

Discussing today if genius is born or made is becoming increasingly futile. But we always have the choice to believe or not to believe. Einstein himself offers us a useful reflection. He was interviewed in the last days of life by a journalist, who wanted to know more about this great genius. He asked Einstein if he thought the world was a friendly or a hostile place. Einstein replied that he did not know but that if a person wants to believe that the world is a friendly place, he will use his discoveries for the support and advancement of humanity. If instead he believes that the world is hostile, he will use the same discoveries to create barriers, to demonstrate his superiority over others and possibly try to destroy them. We contribute to shaping the world we want based on what we believe.

In the same way, according to our way of thinking of whether genius is born or made, when we set out to teach someone or to facilitate their journey of learning, we will automatically be conditioned by what we believe. We may dedicate a lot of energy and care because we think the student can become even more skilful, or we can give our time sparingly, not wasting any more than necessary, because we think they are limited. Or even worse, we can decide not to spend any energy in a certain direction, because, according to Einstein, it is like trying to teach a fish to climb a wall.

If we think that we can become geniuses, we will dedicate ourselves with the utmost effort, clearly not deceiving ourselves that everyone will arrive at the same point because there are too many variables and unforeseen events at stake. But without giving up too quickly and without blaming the other or attributing negative connotations, for example, of being incapable or resistant, we can, in a dignified manner, dedicate ourselves to finding alternative ways to the possible difficulties we encounter in teaching someone something.

One assumption that can help us in these moments is that we have all the resources we need to live and work successfully. Resources are like potential, like seeds, like the acorn that will become an oak. Clearly, this will happen with the care of the gardener who, for their part, will use their resources as well as invoking those of the universe, the sun and the rain to facilitate the growth of the plant. This reflection leads to expand further the previously mentioned assumption. Resources are not necessarily all confined in a single person, but they reside in the system of which we are a part.

The system includes the present, that is, the relationship that is created with other sentient beings, but also the past, how we manage to use the knowledge handed down by previous generations for our enlightenment. The system also includes the future as it encourages us to innovate, to find new solutions.

The first missions in space are a clear testimony of the use of resources, the past through the existing laws of physics, the present in the form of the wealth that resulted from the interaction of a group of dedicated people and the future by means of the dream launched by Kennedy in the early 1960s. It was not necessary to invent a new type of human being, only the acumen to allow these various resources to share the common goal.

The resources are already in the system but need to be reorganized. It is like aligning the digits of a combination lock to open it. It is said that Michelangelo, when asked what he had in mind when faced with a block of stone, replied that he wanted to free the statue that was trapped inside. It is something that can be seen in his unfinished sculptures, for example, the Atlas Slave. The way to free the statue is to remove all that is superfluous, that is, all the stone that is not part of the statue. Can this be a way to free the genius that is in each of us? A genius that can lose their desire when forced to conform, to follow the impositions and dogmas of the context in which they live and to become what others want.

According to epigenetics, that is, how the environment and habits can modify DNA, a good physical workout is important if we want to nurture our resources. It is estimated that 40 minutes of exercise, 3 times a week serve to increase the size of the hippocampus, the part of the brain dedicated to learning and memory. A brisk walk also has a similar effect and it is useful to vary the route from time to time, absorbing the new scenario and memorizing the new path.

Furthermore, starting a new hobby or learning a new piece of music or a foreign language seems to keep the brain active longer.

7 WE LEARN SOMETHING EVERY DAY

When the student is ready, the teacher arrives.

We probably all have the experience of having attempted to learn something new but not succeeding, whether it was a scientific or an artistic subject, a new language or a physical or sports activity. Sometime later, we returned to the same subject, only to marvel at how easy it had become. Maybe we found a more empathic teacher, one that resonated with us, or maybe we got rid of some of the preconceptions that hindered us, thereby allowing us to face the new learning with more openness. It is no coincidence that when the student is ready, as the saying goes, the teacher arrives.

The world is full of stimuli from which we can learn at any time. Every experience, every mood, every encounter with any form of life could be a source of learning. That is, if we do not ignore these moments but see and experience them with new, fresh eyes. And if we do not try to reduce everything new into the category of the already known. Such attitudes die hard, largely due to a sort of pride which manifests itself in not wanting to appear unprepared and incompetent in the face of the great mystery of the universe.

Instead, we can commit ourselves to seeing the same things, even if already known, from new angles. We come to realize, for example, that certain things, certain people who seemed distant and hostile, when contextualized in another frame of reference, or experienced from another mental state are not as they appeared before.

The problem is that we are not always ready for such mental gymnastics. One of the reasons is that we prefer to remain attached to our concept of what is right, keeping our status quo intact. Any new information that comes in, any attempt to learn something new involves a certain destabilization, a risk that some pieces of our castle of certainty will crumble. It is a phenomenon commonly called confusion, often feared and loathed so much so that to say that someone is confused is not by any means a compliment.

From its Latin etymology, to confuse means to melt or to liquefy and it is, therefore, a moment in which our mental structure becomes less solid, less rigid. It is a moment of transition when the information we are receiving has not yet acquired a new solid state, and as a result, we feel we are neither fish nor fowl. These are moments when our sense of self is in a state of transition and, consequently, we cannot express our authenticity. It is the condition of Alice, who when asked by the caterpillar 'Who are you?' replied, 'I really couldn't tell you now. I can tell you who I was when I got up this morning, but since then I think I've changed several times.'

Confusion, therefore, seems to be an essential part of growth. On the condition that we believe that we can still grow, in other words—learn. According to the maxim that we learn something new every day, being alive means we are not complete, we are still a work in progress. It means that we can keep the door open so that the master will be welcome when they show up. This is the inventor's mentality, for example, like that of Thomas Edison. He was the inventor of the incandescent light bulb and succeeded only after thousands of attempts which, he said, were solutions to other problems. Edison had an incredible sense of curiosity. He always asked, 'How does this work?' 'Is there another way to do this?' 'Does this have to be this way?' He was not afraid to ask questions. He was not afraid of uncertainty because, as Anton Chekhov said, 'Only idiots and charlatans think they know and understand everything. Experiencing uncertainty makes us more kind, more creative and more alive.'

It is an attitude that allows us to broaden our horizons. One of the ways to cultivate it is by traveling abroad, immersing ourselves in the uses and customs of the foreign country. Provided that we do not judge, we do not make comparisons between our own customs and those of the other people's. Even without moving geographically, opportunities for learning are not lacking. Any event is a golden moment to learn something new about ourselves. An illness, for example, teaches us how to listen more deeply to our body, an injury makes us understand where to put more attention in the future, a failure invites us to realize where we were not sufficiently prepared. There are so many moments of this kind in our everyday life but we tend not to face them, we prefer to delegate the solution to others, sometimes even invoking destiny. We prefer to live by habit which, at times, is nothing but a kind of mental laziness in which our thoughts of today are mostly the leftovers of yesterday.

Speaking of failures, an example is when in the role of a parent, a teacher, a therapist or simply as a friend we cannot convince another person of our point of view. After much insistence, we should conclude, if we are honest with ourselves, that we have failed, but often we prefer to say that the other person is resistant. We may say, for example, that talking to her is like throwing seeds on cement. It is a conclusion that on the one hand may save us time because it will allow us to dedicate our precious time elsewhere where the soil may be more ready and more fertile, but on the other hand, it limits us, thus, limiting our growth. We are depriving ourselves of a great opportunity to expand our mental map and our possibilities.

If only we could admit that we were not able, that we were not as effective as we would have liked, we could open ourselves to experiment other ways in which our message could arrive. The downside of this approach, however, is that we have to be ready to see some cracks emerge in our carefully guarded castle of certainties, as the much-feared uncertainty and confusion enter. Thankfully, according to Japanese tradition, the crack is what allows light to enter.

In situations like this, the proverbial straw can be turned into gold. What seemed to be worthless, ready to be thrown away can instead be a great moment of learning and growth. The alchemy lies in asking ourselves what the situation is trying to teach us. It is a change of mentality, when we are faced with a difficulty, that can be summarized in the words of Graf von Durkheim,

> The man, who, being really on the Way, falls upon hard times in the world will not, as a consequence, turn to that friend who offers him refuge and comfort and encourages his old self to survive. Rather, he will seek out someone who will faithfully and inexorably help him to risk himself, so that he may endure the suffering and pass courageously through it.[3]

The adverse situation creates a raft that allows us to go to that other shore, beyond the status quo, thereby expanding our repertoire of answers.

---

[3] Karlfried Graf von Durkheim, *The Way of Transformation: Daily Life as Spiritual Practice* (Sandpoint, ID: Morning Light Press, 2006).

Life, it is said, presents itself with everything we need to learn. Whether we stay at home or in office, the master arrives punctually. Everything we do is, therefore, an opportunity for awakening. Referring to the situation in which we related to another person, trying to convince her, some useful questions to ask ourselves could be:

- If the situation or difficulty contained a message to learn something about ourselves, what could be the message?

- What does the situation want to teach us about our capacity to convince and about our dialectical and persuasive skills?

- What part of the other person is the obstacle, and how can we respectfully communicate with this part?

- What stability does the person find through their way of reasoning, and how to ensure they maintain such stability even with a new and different reasoning?

- What are those principles that we do not want to give up while interacting with others, and how can we give less importance to the behaviours and thoughts of others if these do not contrast with or affect our principles?

An additional factor is that when we feel we are not succeeding in our intent we may have a negative emotional reaction, which often forces us to defend ourselves even more strongly, making us feel righteous. However, letting some time pass so that the emotional component, or the amygdala, can rest, we allow the neocortex, the rational brain, to resume its functioning.

'An unexamined life,' said Aristotle, 'is not worth living.' By means of questions, we can review our conclusions, which may sometimes be too hasty, and instead focus our attention on a deeper level than usual. We can let more opinions live together in the same cage, which simply means having a more open mind. We could, thus, be less defensive in the face of challenges when these are not really threatening our survival, only our status quo.

We will, therefore, be able to generate alternative responses with respect to the usual, spontaneous ones. But we must be careful not to settle for less than three alternatives. This is the minimum number that could really lead to new choices, to a new expansion of our horizons and of our ways of thinking. A single alternative could be only the flip side of the same coin and could, therefore, be as rigid as the original way of thinking. Two alternatives, it is said, could lead to the dilemma of never knowing which to actually use. Three would seem to be the minimum number if we want to start working more constructively.

WHEN WE ACCUSE OTHERS

We are not troubled by things but by the view we take of them.

—*Epictetus*

What happens when we accuse someone, maybe even pointing a finger at them? Why are relationships, even the most idyllic ones, prone to be transformed, at any moment, into stormy discussions? It may well be that the other person did or said something that we did not like, but is this enough to blame them and even to try to make them feel ashamed for it?

When we blame someone, it is often an immediate, emotional reaction, not under the control of our faculty of reasoning, almost like an unconditional reflex. Unlike a criticism—which could be more neutral, and goes to say that a behaviour has not met certain criteria, for example, the person did not do what was expected of them—an accusation involves more of the emotional brain. The stronger the accusation, the more we are tempted to point our finger, not just metaphorically, because we perceive the behaviour of the other as a possible threat to our stability. We feel that our mental map, our conception of the world has been threatened and we think we can restore it by accusing the other. We think that by annulling the other, our sense of self will be fuller than theirs. We think that by putting them down, we will seem taller than them.

We can almost certainly appreciate that this thinking is not really a reasoned approach, instead it is more of a reaction. According to neuroscience, there are about six billion cells that are activated every second in the emotional brain, compared to about the 100 stimuli in the rational brain. Consequently, it is rather easy that if we are not prepared, the action of the other could impact us more at an emotional level, thereby making us perceive it as a possible threat to our stability and survival. Our reaction is, therefore, to defend ourselves by attacking or accusing the other.

In this sense, when we accuse, we may just be reacting to defend our status quo. We are perhaps trying to shout to the world that we are right. When we say that a certain behaviour is incomprehensible, or worse still, is typical of animals, we are boasting that we do not or will never behave in a similar way and that we, unlike them, are worthy to call ourselves human beings. It is a reasoning that allows us to feel virtuous, to feel that we are on the right path, beyond and above those who are at fault. Sometimes it is also a sense of domination, being in control over others and of life in general. This type of scaffolding, without a doubt, makes us feel good but risks degenerating into campaigns of hate against those who have done wrong. And we begin to rage against the sinner, risking even to forget what was the sin that was committed.

Similar things happen even at a domestic level. A person in whom we placed our appreciation and trust behaves in an unexpected way and we are led to accuse them. Even in these situations, we need to be clear whether we are really condemning the action or the person. Sometimes, the accusation arises from our disappointment for not having realized that everyone is fragile in their own particular way. In these circumstances, we can say, according to the Pogo cartoon, 'we have met the enemy, and he is us.' Our self-esteem risks wavering, and we are unable to forgive ourselves but become hard on ourselves and, consequently, on the other person as well. Again, it is the emotional brain that takes over.

According to the latest neuroscientific research, these immediate reactions are the result of changes in our biochemistry. After about 90 seconds, however, the reaction will have run its course and, therefore, if we are still in an altered and hijacked state, it is because we are choosing, consciously or unconsciously, to prolong the thoughts that keep the emotional reaction alive. If we could let the anger and indignation wash off, we will be able to reason and to face the situation in a more balanced way.

If 90 seconds are not enough to regain this state, we can facilitate it by means of some expedients. For example, we can imagine interposing a filter, of glass or of plexiglass, between us and the event so as to see it with eyes that would be less contaminated by the emotions. Another way to free ourselves from the emotional hijack is to imagine ourselves as a journalist or as a reporter, in other words, as a more neutral figure, whose task is only to comment on the situation.

At this point, we can ask ourselves which is more important, the interpersonal relationship or proving that we were right. We can also ask ourselves if we really have all the data that we need to be able to judge. The answer would be obvious; it is said that if we could really know the secret lives even of our enemies, we will find, in everyone's life, enough pain and suffering to disarm any hostility. We will take things on a less personal level, and we will realize that not all the wrongs of the world are necessarily against us. We can then ask ourselves what new choices we have to manage the interaction. Similarly, if the situation involves the society, we can ask ourselves if it is more useful to intervene immediately, risking, however, that this becomes a personal battle or if it would be more appropriate to do something else so that any future social interactions may become more constructive.

When we are in a state of greater neutrality, that is, when the rational brain has resumed its work, we can also identify what were the stimuli, the so-called triggers, that may have provoked our reaction. We can ask ourselves what we saw, heard or felt just before reacting, that is, what, on a subjective level, triggered our reaction. This way of analysing, taking distance and reviewing those moments almost in slow motion allows us to be more ready to anticipate and, therefore, manage an emotional outbreak the next time we feel the internal tension rising.

In addition to reasoning, we can also bring some comfort to the part that was so stimulated by those triggers as to provoke an exaggerated reaction. We may imagine that the event created an injury in us to which we can give the necessary attention. It would, therefore, be useful to identify where this wounded part may lie within us. This will not be a search for a physical part, visible on the operating table, but it will be more of a metaphorical sense of this presence. For example, when we speak about a lump in our throat, it is not that we are referring to something physical but to a feeling about the energy that has been trapped in this area. The same reasoning applies when we talk about a knot in the stomach, a stab in the back, a weight on the shoulders and other similar metaphors. Each of these indicates an organic or physical place where we perceive something that unfortunately does, sometimes, translates into illness. If the part does not present itself spontaneously, we can find it by scanning the body, imagining that a light comes in when we have located the area. Once identified, we can then take a few breaths to regain balance and centre ourselves while visualizing that we are breathing air that is enriched with affection and caresses that we are directing towards the suffering part.

Another level where accusation rears its head is when the other person behaves in a way that we ourselves would have liked to behave but could not. This is an interpretation that is often diffi-cult to accept, precisely because we deny the important fact that many of our parts live in an area technically called the shadow. This area contains all those behaviours that, in the early years of our life, might not have received approval from parents and educators and so have been relegated to live in the dark corners of our being. When we said bad words, for example, we were often forced to take them back. If we expressed intentions of wanting to hurt our little brother, they told us that we had to love him because hate was not allowed. So, we were obliged to silence certain emotions rather than owning them and pro-cessing them. We hid them under the doormat, hoping to have got rid of them forever. But instead the emotion continued to live hidden inside us. Thus, when another person expresses one of those behaviours that we have repressed, their action becomes, sometimes, a mirror for us. It is a mirror that reminds us of and, in some way, reactivates that part of us with which we have not come to terms, made peace, a neglected part that still needs to be recognized, accepted and managed. As it is dif-ficult to point our finger at ourselves, mainly because we do not know where to point it, we find ourselves accusing the other person precisely because they are recalling a part of us.

What can we do with a neglected part? It is like asking what to do with a child who has been neglected, perhaps, an adopted child who could not benefit from parental love. The answer would seem quite obvious, namely, to give affection, a lot of affection, not to prostrate ourselves, not to expiate for what has been missing but to allow them to feel more integrated. The same goes for those neglected parts of us. We can imagine them as a child, fragile and incapable of managing themselves adequately in society, a child who had been forced to remain silent to conform to the will of adults.

Martin Luther King said that we must be faithful to our principles, and at the same time sensitive to those who do not agree with us. In this way, there is nothing that cannot be achieved. We can train that sensitivity that will allow us to behave more appropriately, even in situations of great conflict, without necessarily falling into the trap of accusation, and clearly without abandoning our principles.

The true miracle, it is said, is not so much walking on water but walking on this earth, being able to meet common everyday challenges.

9 WHEN THE INTENTION IS POSITIVE

Something unknown is doing we don't know what.

—*Arthur Eddington*

What to do when a person or a group of people carries out a violent deed, for example, a massacre, something that is becoming an increasingly common phenomenon in today's world? What to do when a person commits a socially unacceptable action? One of the first reactions that comes to many people's minds is to condemn that person, worse yet, to hate them. This is, however, a strongly impulsive reaction, the consequence of which could be to incite and perpetuate a cycle of anger and hatred, the same factors that most likely triggered the action or the massacre in the first place.

When we allow ourselves a little time to peek just below the surface, we come to realize that any behaviour is the result of many factors. Some of these refer to our past, in other words, how we were educated and raised. An example that, unfortunately, is still heard, perhaps a little less often today, is that when a child complains that one of their companions has beaten them, the parent responds by asking them if they returned the offense with even more force. This is the type of education that, if not updated, could easily lead to acts of aggression and adult violence.

Other factors refer to the present and are, for example, the emotional states that we go through during the day and, above all, how we experience them. When everything is calm and we do not feel at risk we manage the challenges that arise in the most appropriate way. But if we perceive a situation as a threat, the part of the brain called the amygdala is activated and we react principally by running away or by fighting. These are ways of behaving that we have inherited or learned since our youth, a sort of automatic pilot that makes us act on impulse, not leaving us the time to reflect on the consequences of our actions.

Still, other factors, again below the surface, refer to the future, to the expectations we have based on the behaviour we are planning to implement. We wonder if our action will bring us gratification but, unfortunately, this reflection is often short-sighted. This is because it is a gratification aimed particularly at ourselves, neglecting the effect on others and on the extended context in which we are participating. It is a gratification connected to our survival, the classic mode of the predator, which we still carry within us ever since the era of the reptiles.

These are just some of the factors that contribute to keep intact our 'house of cards', that delicate scaffolding, sometimes, very precarious but which is the basis of our way of being, our thoughts and consequently of our behaviour. It is the castle that we always aim to maintain as it is and the simplest, least expensive way of doing so is to resist any attempt to update or change it. We want to maintain our status quo in order to rediscover the stability, security and the happiness that our comfort zone has provided and which we hope it will continue to offer us. Our cardinal points, that is, our values continue to keep us on a familiar, well-mapped and consolidated route so much so that new information is often refused or deformed so as to confirm that our mental map of the world is the right one. These are the situations in which people find it difficult to admit they are wrong, for fear of seeing their house of cards collapse.

So, let us explore what positive intention is all about. It refers to everything we do to maintain our status quo intact and to prove to ourselves that we are not going against our values. We take the liberty to express ourselves in this way, and we do not give ourselves permission to go beyond the boundaries of our usual ways of thinking and acting. We, thus, risk hurting others because we are so committed to maintaining our own stability that we are not able to reflect appropriately. We are not open to new points of view, new considerations, especially those that can modify the effect of our actions on others.

An analogy is that of the three monkeys, where one does not see, the other does not hear and the other does not speak. Sometimes, we do not see and we do not hear because we find ourselves with our eyes and ears covered, due to our perceptive filters, those things we take for granted as the truth. As a result, allowing the mouth to speak or the hands to act, we say things and we perform actions that could harm others and the community.

For example, a person accustomed to a model of blind obedience, perhaps 'inherited' from their family of origin, could have adopted this as the only model that works or the model on which to fall back when other approaches do not work. As a result, finding themselves in a situation of conflict with someone who is hierarchically superior, this person may feel obliged, even if not in agreement, to follow the orders from above and even adopt them as their own. Or they may want to repeat the same model that they learned, in turn demanding obedience from others, thus, showing off their strength, raising their voice, forcing their point of view or even physically intervening on others. They could, however, express themselves by reacting, and not by choice, in exactly the opposite way, that is, by being exceedingly accommodating just to show that they are not propagating the model that they had to undergo. In this case, they may overlook many things losing the clear distinction between what is right and what is wrong.

Another very important consideration is that when a person violates social customs, maybe, it is because they are going through a difficult period. Perhaps, they feel alienated, not integrated, their self-esteem is at a historic low and through their incorrect actions, they try to regain a bit of power that, in their opinion, will give them back the self-esteem that was missing. It is easy to understand how a person who feels weak and fragile, to get out of this state, could do the first thing that comes to their mind without reasoning. And if this reflection seems strange, it is enough to reflect how many times we ourselves have behaved in this way. The hope is that, when this is over, we will be able to recover and without looking for a culprit on whom to unload our responsibilities, we could admit that we did not have all the pieces of the picture. Above all, we could ask ourselves how we could have done better in that situation and in similar situations. Without such a reflection, it is more than likely that the next time a similar situation crops up we will behave again as before.

We need to create an adequate space for reflection, a space that is not offered by the conventional punitive systems in force. Punishment, though it may derive from a call to return to fundamental and universal values, for example, justice, is often because of the hurry to point our finger and to accuse. This makes us feel exempt from examining our own behaviour. If we were to do so, it would be like pointing the finger at ourselves. But it is much easier to point it towards others. Even though this is the attitude of the ostrich, the intention, as explained, is positive. It is to avoid the difficulty of having to discover our responsibility and the consequent embarrassment in finding the answer.

Understanding the positive intention allows us to condemn the sin, not the sinner. The so-called sinner may still feel part of the society, their self-esteem will not be tarnished and they will not need to fabricate defences for their actions, perhaps, retreating into the belief that they did the right thing. When the positive intention is understood, the person could feel more ready to review their wrong behaviour in a more evolved and intelligent way.

It would be useful, from the age in which one can reason, to explain that destructive actions can have negative consequences on others. Instead of correcting the child by slapping them, or the adult by casting them into prison, it could be useful to take the person aside, if necessary segregating them, if we see that he has a marked tendency to commit antisocial acts, and in the meantime, educate them. A useful question to ask a person who did something socially inappropriate is, 'If this was done to you, what would your reaction be.' Surely the question by itself does not suffice as a solution, it is necessary to continually make sure that each person feels sufficiently gratified and satisfied, not to have to fall back on antisocial behaviour. For an adult, this could be the opportunity to feel integrated, useful, perhaps through a job. For everyone, it will definitely also be a question of recreating self-esteem that may have been lost at some point in their life journey.

How can we stop the temptation of an eye for an eye, a tooth for a tooth and instead put ourselves in the shoes of someone who committed an infraction so as to recognize their positive intention, and to think, 'If I were them, I probably would have done the same thing?' We can ponder on the delicate balance in them that broke, the pain that person was carrying inside themselves that exploded into an antisocial behaviour. Can we reason in this way for people close to us, people far from us, even for people we don't know? A key is compassion, understood not as pity but as how much suffering the person is carrying within themselves. When we are genuinely in their shoes, we can understand better what suffering is because we realize how many burdens we too have to carry.

By accepting the concept of a positive intention, we can understand many of the limitations of others and, above all, ours, and instead of living in the regime of an inner dictator, we can find, with courage, alternative ways to free ourselves from the grip of past, present and future conditionings and live more in harmony with ourselves and with others.

10

LANGUAGE INFLUENCES THOUGHT

If thought corrupts language, language can also corrupt thought.

—George Orwell

Games of word associations are very entertaining as well as illuminating and we never cease to wonder how from one word we can get to another that, at first glance, might seem in no way related. It all happens thanks to the neural connections in the brain, the synapses, which are responsible for making sense of what is happening around us. The information that arrives from the world follows a pathway in the brain, a track, which, in order to survive, must connect to another, and to many others, and in this intricate design of connections we begin to make sense, that is, we succeed in drawing the appropriate conclusions about what to think, what to say and how to act.

Sometimes, the connections are not immediate, and we must rummage through our memory. Technically, this is called a transderivational search and is a result of exploration into our deep structure. It requires the brain to interrogate an immense number of synaptic connections in order to understand which path to take or what sense to make of the incoming information. It is also one of the fundamental bases in hypnosis especially regarding the school of Milton Erickson, the doctor who was most responsible for re-launching hypnosis as a therapeutic approach. The hypnotic process, by triggering a transderivational search, manages to touch parts of our experience that have remained submerged but are still present, conditioning or influencing our actions in the present. Erickson recalled that the effect of words can last even for several decades and this has been widely demonstrated in several circumstances.

Poets, in particular, know that the use of one word rather than another conditions the thought of the reader. For this reason, it would be absurd, despite still being done in some academic environments, to try to give unique interpretations to poetry, since each person is influenced in their own particular way. We are corrupted, to use the language of George Orwell, in a very subjective manner. Words will touch sections of our experience that are connected to pleasant or unpleasant emotions and can, therefore, influence our emotional sphere. These reactions may only be partly shared, for example, by people belonging to the same culture.

By way of experimentation, if we ask someone to think about mom and dad and to say the words 'mother, mom, my mom, father, dad, my dad' one after another, leaving a small pause for reflection after each word so that the neural connections can become active, it is very likely that with a little attention we will notice some variations, even slight ones, but still important, regarding the emotional state of the person. We can see where their gaze goes, how the complexion of their face changes, what small facial tensions emerge, how their tone of voice changes, all factors that indicate they are going through particular emotional states as they say these words. We can do a similar experiment on ourselves, thinking of words or saying them out aloud and being mindful, in other words, more internally aware of what 'corruptions' are in progress.

The following three verbs are examples that are common to many people of how language can strongly influence our thinking, and how the limits of our language, according to the great philosopher Ludwig Wittgenstein, become the limits of our world.

HELP

This is a word that is commonly used but it is necessary to think that in the process of helping there is probably a person who is more fortunate and one who is less so. A relationship of this type could, therefore, arise during our everyday use of the word. If so, help becomes a relationship of one-upmanship, superiority–inferiority. In a sense, this is the way some gifts are given. In the collaborative tradition of the Kalahari people, giving is a gesture that means wanting to continue a relationship of friendship, while in the competitive style in some parts of New Guinea and in the Potlach tradition of British Columbia, giving is a gesture of superiority that puts the recipient in a condition of inferiority in which they know a priori that they will not be able to match the gift received. This is also a consideration that we all, in our daily lives, can determine to what extent is true when giving or receiving a gift.

When such a mentality is established, namely that the recipient is in a state of deficit, the risk is that of continuing to propagate and strengthen their condition of incapacity thereby creating a situation similar to addiction. The receiver continues to wait to receive help or, in some cases, demands it without realizing that if they really want to improve their present uncomfortable condition, it is them who will have to act differently. The condition of waiting and hoping is one that still prevails in several underdeveloped countries.

In slightly more developed countries, another phenomenon occurs, again, linked to aid. Stemming certainly from the positive intention to alleviate the suffering of those who seem to barely survive by their own means of sustenance, or perhaps presuming, wrongly, that this is so, help is given, but this ends up stifling the local economy. The receiver, as is seen today in some parts of the world, would be able to generate wealth on their own if they were less invaded both by tangible help and, indirectly, through certain initiatives, for example, in the Christmas period, in favour of certain populations. It is an example of the saying, 'the road to evil is paved with good intentions, whereas the road to goodness is paved with good deeds.'

If we want to extend ourselves towards other people or populations, we can begin to redefine the action of helping, by using another verb, for example, assisting, accompanying, supporting, facilitating, guiding or any other verb that recognizes the other as a person of equal dignity and possibilities. These are verbs that have the sense of teaching how to fish, not just giving fish to the allegedly hungry.

FIGHT

This is a verb that has a strong emotional impact. As we think of wars, we can reflect, in this precise moment, on the impact the word 'war' has on us. Inevitably, we are led to think about a conquest, eradication of the enemy, annihilation of resistance in which one party emerges as a winner, glorious, without having to fear any future emergence of conflicts. Not by chance, the same word continues to be used in campaigns against diseases, evoking conquests by one party while the other has to lay down their arms.

But all this may conceal a terrible deception. By definition, a struggle involves more than one party and it is normal that each will want to strengthen itself to be able to dominate the other. A country defeated in a war will hardly lay down their arms but will strive to rise again and this may well happen in unexpected ways and in unexpected moments.

The same goes for our body too. If we attribute a form of intelligence to our cells, the risk is that they too will want to strengthen themselves to avoid being defeated. This triggers a mechanism that could be costly and endless. It is common to hear about winning the battle but not the war and one could see cases in which a disease seems to have disappeared only to resurface in another part of the body, perhaps after some time. Even bacteria, today, with the use of increasingly strong antibiotics seem to want to resist these bombardments, creating variations in their structure that make them seemingly invincible.

The desire to heal means regaining a situation of wholeness, that is, wholeness in the body and in the soul. This means that mind and body are collaborating towards the same goal and, above all, each supports the other. It also means that the person is reintegrated into the environment in which they live, which includes their family as well as the wider group, that is, friends, animals, if any, and other sentient beings.

Noticing the effect of these thoughts on our emotional state, what verbs come to mind as we talk about healing? Verbs that will certainly be less spectacular than 'fighting' but could have a far more interesting beneficial effect. Some are harmonizing, optimizing, feeling good and becoming more whole.

TRY TO

When we try to do something, whether it be homework or a test, it is like making an attempt. Trying and attempting are words that seem to bring to mind a real possibility of failure. In spite of this, we often hear people telling perhaps their children or their collaborators to try to do things in a certain way. We want to encourage them to do something, especially to go beyond what is known, beyond the status quo, but it is like pressing the accelerator and the brake pedal of a car at the same time. We are inviting someone to do something, but at the same time we are also evoking a significant possibility of failure inherent in the concept of trying. Our conscious, rational part knows that it must strive to perform the action, but the unconscious part, without our realizing it, is not convinced of succeeding. The person finds themselves struggling more, instead of acting fluently, with the consequence of tiring quickly.

Using this way of communicating also means making a person involuntarily less accountable for their successes and, in particular, for their failures. Telling someone to try to do something indirectly means telling them not to be too engaged, since the possibility of success is only fifty-fifty, in other words, a lot will be left to chance. Whoever succeeds could only have done so because they were lucky.

One of the reasons we say to try to do something is because we fear that if we were to be more assertive in saying to do something, we could seem too directive and invasive, running the risk of imposing our will on the other. All this is true to the extent that we have not taken the time to create a good interpersonal relationship that would render the exhortation less directive. We have not taken the time to figure out who is our interlocutor, what are their difficulties and to feel ourselves somehow involved and co-responsible.

Sometimes, saying to try is also a way of not accepting our responsibility. Maybe because we want to feel more appreciated, like a sort of magician, ready to dispense advice which we are not even sure of. We launch messages urging someone to try to do something, hiding behind the fact that if they do not work, they were just trials.

A useful suggestion comes from Yoda, the mythical figure of Jedi wisdom in the *Star Wars* saga. He reminds us, 'Do or do not, there is no try.'

11 BEING OF GOOD SUPPORT

Alone we can do so little; together we can do so much.

—*Helen Keller*

In Greek mythology, one of the best-known figures of support was Mentor. Ulysses, preparing for his departure to Troy, entrusted Mentor with his home and with the education of his son, Telemachus. Mentor's task was to teach Ulysses' son all he knew. He did this by presenting himself in different guises in times of need. Another figure of support, equally well known, was Chiron who, besides being one of the founders of medicine, was Achilles' guide, always present to look after his education and his growth. These supporting relationships are repeated even today, in the form of parents, leaders, therapists, educators or even just trustworthy friends.

Every time we enter this territory, we approach one of the great unknowns of life, namely the diversity of our interlocutor. We never know what really happens in their mind, we never really know why their mental map is different from ours, whether that be very much or just a little. We know that they also use the classic mechanisms of transformation that contribute towards the creation of their own map, as described in the chapter 'The Tip of the Iceberg'. We do not know, however, unless we are good at guessing, which pieces of input from the world they choose to generalize, delete or deform. It may, therefore, be a good start, if we want to be supportive, to think that if we were in their shoes, maybe, we would use these mechanisms exactly as they do.

This is a good way to open ourselves to another person. It is a way of holding the space in which that person's thoughts can breathe by being expressed instead of continuing to reverberate inside their head. Holding the space does not mean agreeing but providing an environment, through our attitude, that is adequately safe, protected and stimulating in which, metaphorically, a young plant can nourish itself and grow. It is a sort of container, a *temenos,* a word that comes from Greek and refers to the ground that is singled out and reserved, a compassionate ground in which what is harmful, what is no more of use and is outdated can 'die' in order to make way for something new to be born. It is a space in which, according to writer Henri Nouwen's *Reaching Out,* 1975, people are encouraged to disarm themselves, lay aside their occupations and pre-occupations and listen with attention and care to the voices speaking in their centre. And we know that within our centre lies the source of creativity and of new solutions.

But how is it more useful to respond, if we want to be supportive, like a sort of mentor, when the other person tells us about a problem of theirs? We can be curious, not to indulge in gossip but to be curious in a more scientific way, that restless and relentless desire to know and, therefore, to explore, allowing more information to come to the surface. Or we can close ourselves, turn away, maybe, start to accuse the person saying they shouldn't or it is not good to have problems like that. In such cases, it is as if their situation is acting as a mirror for us. They may be touching a part of ours that we have ignored and their story does nothing but bring us back to when we were in the grip of a problem that we have perhaps too hastily put aside.

It may also happen that our interlocutor breaks down into a valley of tears. This situation, for many, is somewhat embarrassing; we feel touched in our heartstrings by the problem that the other is experiencing. Maybe, we hasten to give aid through a hug, some consolation or advice, a handkerchief—all manifestations that we may be uncomfortable in the presence of someone's pain. It is not easy, although it would be more useful, to let the person liberate themselves from the situation of despair by crying. We fear, perhaps, that a broken heart will lead to a broken person. We forget that pain is part of growth, it is not some kind of evil that is possessing the person.

It is useful in these circumstances to be able to differentiate between ourselves and the other. It is commonly heard that the problem is not ours, it's theirs, not to mean that the person is the problem, but that they are currently going through a situation that is all about them, even though it might remind us of aspects of our life. If we want to pay good attention, we must be able to know we can take appropriate distance from the situation in order to put things into a more useful perspective. This is the capacity of differentiating without dissociating, separating ourselves without feeling separated, something that does not come too easily because when we are aware of the differences between us and others, we risk starting to feel like strangers towards them, we may begin to condemn them, segregate and exclude them. Taking an appropriate distance from the situations that others are experiencing is extremely useful and is something we can practise on a daily basis. We can observe how each person walks, how they dress, how they speak and recognize that there are differences in behaviours between one person and another. Without judging, criticizing or condemning we can appreciate how many different ways there are to express our humanity.

At times, the difficulty in opening up to problems of the other is related to the mentality that does not tolerate our falling, our failure and when we see it in our interlocutor, we cannot tolerate it even in them. A useful reflection at this point is that if we were not able to fall or to fail, it would mean that we are not alive, that we are statues made of granite, something like the pyramids. Surely, this is not a nice thought but, in some moments, a sense of guilt and shame for our failures was instilled in us and this attitude continues to influence our ways of being and of seeing reality. But being alive means, we can fall and unlike the pyramids, which if they were knocked down would only become dust, we can rise up again. We can be as resilient as the great coral reef that has rebuilt itself five times over the last 30 thousand years.

The supporting relationship, when it is of the superiority–inferiority type, becomes a helping one. With the need to offer solutions, we risk imprisoning the other in our own point of view. We risk curtailing the other's development, always giving the metaphorical fish rather than allowing the person to learn how to fish. When the relationship is instead of the inferiority–superiority type, there will be a kind of reverential fear towards the other. The temptation, in this case, is to accept anything that arises, not stimulating a good reflection concerning the appropriateness and correctness of the choices. This is the condition of the saviour, who comes to someone's aid whenever they see others in difficulty. A third dysfunctional attitude is when the one who wants to be supportive finds themselves in a hopeless condition. In this case, they would feel as if they were a victim of circumstances, and the thought would be that any attempt to improve is useless because 'nothing works'.

The attitude of being of support can be summarized in this poem by Rumi.

Come, come, whoever you are.
Wanderer, worshiper, lover of leaving.
It doesn't matter.
Ours is not a caravan of despair.
Come, even if you have broken your vows a thousand times.
Come, yet again, come, come.

In conclusion, what is needed to be of good support, to be a mentor for another person is to be as open as possible, silencing our own internal voices so as to leave the space where something interesting can sprout and grow. William Blake, the English poet, wrote that lies are born when we look into the eyes of others and not through their eyes. This is an invitation to widen our gaze so as to perceive more of a situation, resonating with more parts of our interlocutor's mental map. And with the wise use of some questions, we can be pleasantly surprised when we discover much more than we thought possible.

LISTENING

Tell a wise person or else keep silent.

—Johann Goethe

In a world dominated by words, as witnessed by the popularity of talk shows, it won't surprise us so much to know that one of the most sought-after skills, precisely because it is slowly disappearing, is that of listening. And, as the Greek philosopher Zeno said, the reason we have two ears and one mouth is to listen more and talk less. When we listen, maybe we get to learn something, we expand our knowledge both in terms of the facts of life as well as in matters regarding the people with whom we are relating. In the latter case, we will be more equipped to offer valid support to those who may be in such need.

The art and science of listening involves paying particular attention. This does not regard only the words but, above all, the non-verbal messages concerning the body and the paraverbal ones relating to the voice. These are the carrier waves on which most of the 'real' meanings of the words are nested, camouflaged and hidden and these meanings are, generally speaking, specific to each person. Only in the few cases of culturally recognizable gestures can we speak of a common meaning, for example, nodding, shaking the head, thumb facing up or down, to name a few. To understand other gestures, we need to tune in as much as possible to the other person, thus, minimizing the possibility of losses, distractions, blockages and breaks in the transmission or of projecting our own interpretations onto the content. In some shamanic traditions, it is important for the healer to tune in so deeply to the patient as to be able to guess the nature of the problem that the patient is experiencing even before any verbal exchange.

One of the main reasons that makes listening difficult is its reputation for being unproductive and not very serious in several work cultures. We are not doing anything concrete, tangible and measurable when we listen, and few perceive a salary increase thanks to listening. As soon as a problem arises, someone will, almost certainly, urge the other to do something. We are not trained to listen. This is a reflection that does not apply to mothers, who are generally more capable because they had to listen deeply to ensure the survival of their children. It is understandable how such a skill is underestimated in a male-dominated society.

In his work *The Art of Listening*, the Indian philosopher Krishnamurti, about the difficulty of listening, said,

> I do not know if you have ever examined how you listen, it doesn't matter to what, whether to a bird, to the wind in the leaves, to the rushing waters, or how you listen to a dialogue with yourself, to your conversation in various relationships with your intimate friends, your wife or husband. If we try to listen we find it extraordinarily difficult, because we are always projecting our opinions and ideas, our prejudices, our background, our inclinations, our impulses; when they dominate we hardly listen to what is being said. In that state there is no value at all. One listens and therefore learns, only in a state of attention, a state of silence in which this whole background is in abeyance, is quiet; then, it seems to me, it is possible to communicate.[4]

---

[4] Jiddu Krishnamurti, *The Art of Listening* (Ojai, CA: Krishnamurti Foundation America, 2019).

Even when the listener remains silent, however, it can often be seen that they are ready to intervene as soon as the other party pauses for a breath. It means that they didn't really listen but were just letting the others finish while they were planning and gathering up energy for their reply. This type of listening can be compared to the habit of over-marking in dogs who not only mark their territory, but also cover the one already marked by others. And that is also the difference between a debate or a discussion, in which everyone wants to defeat the other's point of view, and a dialogue, where the goal is to find a richer sense by integrating the opinions of all parties concerned.

A listener who really wants to receive what the other is offering must remain in silence. It is not a silence of indifference but it is like a container for the other. A container that offers a protected, nourishing space that encourages the person to express themselves. To facilitate good listening, it is useful that there is a strong component of interest in what the other has to say, especially how they put together the pieces of their reasoning as well as respect, understood as believing that the interlocutor is a person of value, worthy of being heard. This is the sense, in the Chinese ideogram for listening, composed of different characters, one of which is the king. The listener, especially with regards to the speaker, has a decisive role which is to stimulate them to tell their best narrative.

Good listening, which derives from the practices of coaching and therapeutic listening, can be divided into the following three phases:

1. **Recognition:** This can be achieved from a centred state, which allows us to give all our attention to the interlocutor so as to receive and welcome them.

Some suggestions to facilitate this phase are:

a. Imagine that the other is capable, even if not immediately, of coming to terms with their own issues.
b. Imagine being a catalyst in their process of clarification.
c. We position our body towards the other as if it were a container.
d. Calibrate and reflect some salient elements of their body posture, without mimicking them.
e. This means placing our body in a mirror position with respect to theirs.
f. Resist, at first, any temptation to give advice.
g. Nod from time to time to give the other permission to continue talking.

2. **Acceptance:** This second phase is that of being interested in the other and is a further key phase to facilitate listening. It is about accepting what the person is saying, maybe repeating their words or their key concepts so that both parties can verify that listening is proceeding without omissions or distortions. It is not a question of agreeing but only letting the content of the other enter, as well as the subtle energy under their words, in order to find the deeper meaning in what they are saying.

3. **Appreciation:** This is the most delicate phase, but it will be very natural if the first two have been carried out well. It is a question of appreciating their positive intention, that is, taking for granted that they have good reasons that motivate what they are saying. It is an appreciation which can be felt or even expressed verbally and only then can we proceed to expand or contradict what we hear.

People tend to really feel heard only when they reach the third level, that of appreciation. And it is a type of listening that is difficult to find in everyday life both at work and in the family. Being able to apply it is a good deed that everyone can do to others, something from which the donor also benefits.

The following anonymous poem illustrates the meaning of listening very eloquently.

When I ask you to listen to me
and you start giving me advice
you are not doing what I asked of you.
When I ask you to listen to me
and you start telling me why I shouldn't have certain reactions
you are treading upon my feelings
When I ask you to listen to me
and you feel you must do something to solve my problems
you aren't of support to me.
Maybe that's why prayers work for some people.
The gods are mute
they don't offer advice
they don't try to fix things
They just listen, and trust that you will find a solution.
Please listen to me
And if you really wish to speak
wait a few minutes
and I promise I'll listen to you.

As we may gather from this poem, listening is an incredibly effective way of empowering another. It is that container of silence which allows a person to re-elaborate his or her internal map of reality, hopefully updating it, bringing it more in harmony with the external world. Listening, in this sense, may be considered a divine gift in which we offer a major part of ourselves to another sentient being.

LISTENING AT DIFFERENT LEVELS

Authentic listening is transformational, it allows us to generate answers that we did not imagine could exist.

According to the tradition of Kundalini yoga, which belongs to the Indian millennial wisdom, the human body contains a series of 'divine' energy points called chakras. Traveling from the base of the spine up to the crown of the head, we find seven chakras each of which is responsible for a specific energy configuration. When these points are awakened, they bring greater integrity and balance to our body.

The first chakra, known as the base or root chakra, is found precisely at the base of the spine and refers to the energy that supports life, that is, survival and primary instincts. The second chakra is that of creativity and is located in the womb—the area responsible for the generation of new life. The third is that of power and is found in the area around the navel. It includes the solar plexus and is responsible for the digestion not only of food, but also of complex concepts, reducing them to more manageable bits. The fourth chakra refers to the heart, the seat of emotions, and is an aspect that distinguishes us from many animals. The fifth is in the throat, the place from which we speak our truth, and, therefore, refers to who we are, in other words our identity. The sixth chakra is that of the third eye, the eye of wisdom, while the seventh is called the crown chakra and it is the area which puts us as one with the rest of the universe.

Some of these chakra points can be roughly equated to the neurological levels, an important contribution of Robert Dilts to the field of neurolinguistic programming (NLP) in 1988. The six neurological levels are, starting from the bottom and going upwards, that of the environment, followed by the level of actions and behaviours, going up to the level of abilities, then values, following up to identity and finally to the level of systemic vision.

The art of listening authentically can be represented in all seven chakras and, analogously, at all the NLP levels. Following is a description of how I operate as a listener in my profession. The reader is invited to immerse themselves in this narrative, and to take away what they consider useful, adapting it to their own style and character. They can, therefore, discard what seems too remote, remembering, however, to challenge themselves to do something that is not usual, something that will lead them gently out of their comfort zone. Going beyond our status quo is, perhaps, the only real way to learn and improve.

The first thing a good listener does, even before dealing with someone, is to take a moment to free themselves from the thoughts and concerns that could impede listening. This can be done by taking a few breaths to bring a state of silence and inner stillness. Then, maintaining this silence, and acting at the level of the first chakra, the environment in NLP, the listener begins to perceive the interlocutor, not as a single person who is dissociated from the rest of the world but as someone who belongs to a context. In this context, one of their priorities, inherited from the animal world, is to look after their survival. It might be useful to imagine that the person brings their uniqueness with them, like a backpack containing their past, significant moments experienced, their family of origin, the present, the state of mind in which they are and the future, that is, their expectations and dreams.

At the level of the second chakra, that of behaviour and creativity, the listener desires to facilitate the emergence of a useful connection, a good relationship between self and the other. For this to happen, they will gradually or quickly place themselves in the other's shoes. The aim is to understand better the nuances of their experience, the subtle energy with which they convey their words. This is a phase that can be facilitated during the exchange of pleasantries because being of light impact they allow us to dedicate more attention to the interlocutor, the position of their body, gestures and tone of voice. The listener can employ some proven techniques, for example, mirroring certain nonverbal and paraverbal aspects. Pleasantries also serve to create a container that welcomes the interlocutor into a protected space, where they can feel free to express themselves.

Going up to the level of the third chakra, which refers to the ability to break down complexity into more manageable pieces, the listener will go beyond duality, beyond seeing a person completely different from themselves. Regardless of the appearance of the interlocutor, the listener wants to be able to see them in their entirety which, according to the Ubuntu tradition, can be expressed in the phrase 'I see you.' These three simple, and at the same time extremely profound words, mean to see the other person under the surface, just like ourselves, that is, a person who rejoices, a person who has satisfactions and also delusions and sadness. The listener does not judge, and this attitude allows them to welcome the interlocutor with great openness. Their mind, clear of thoughts and emptied from preconceptions and expectations, allows the other's contents to resonate inside themselves, thus, facilitating a good climate and good listening.

At this stage, a deeper and often more intimate relationship with the other person begins. The relationship will probably be of a compassionate nature; in any case, there will be a connection and a degree of greater intimacy. It would be essential to experience fully this connection as a moment of significant interdependence. The two people, according to Bateson, become significant parts in the weave of the total complex, in which each part influences the other; and through a process called structural coupling, they are creating a reality that is continuously changing. This is a sign of good communication.

For some, it is like being in the same boat, the boat of life, fragile, destined to sink, hopefully only after having come to terms with some of our worries. Curiosity is very strong, as is the attention with which we listen and ask questions. The interlocutor may begin to feel as if contained in a cocoon of goodness.

Studies in the field of neuroscience confirm that when two people meet, even for a brief moment, the configuration of each of their brains changes. Each influences the other and it is important that this influence can be facilitating, not impeding. It is a mysterious and unique moment, no one knows what the outcome will be, no one knows where it will lead, so it is important to experience it to the fullest.

This is the time when certain belief or beliefs are expressed through attitudes and not just through words. The listener will be very present in the heart chakra, which is also the level of values. Connecting at this level means being aware that every choice of life is not just a rational moment, it is not about dominating every problematic situation, but it is also about savouring the mystery in which we are living. The listener is intent on valuing, giving importance to what the interlocutor communicates. They know this is a propitious moment when no one knows for sure what will be born, but whatever arises will surely have an effect on the future. It is a future that does not yet exist but that is being incubated in every moment of authentic listening, thanks to the two people who are the co-creators of their future and who, consequently, are contributing to the future of the world.

At the level of the fifth chakra, that of identity, the listener can describe themselves through different metaphors. One of these is a midwife, whose job is to facilitate the delivery of ideas, ensuring that they are born appropriately and that they will have sufficient voice to influence the future. Often, conversations between two people serve only to show who is right, who is more powerful in demonstrating their ideas. In good listening, it is useful to think that every person, irrespective of how different they may be, is laying the bases for building something that once integrated with the thought of the listener can become a solid foundation. Maybe, the thought of one person alone is too fragile to survive in isolation, but when coupled with another thought, it could acquire an appropriate robustness that will allow the person to travel more easily through life. And this may also benefit the listener. After all, a high tide is able to raise all the boats in the harbour.

It is worth noting that, like Socrates, the obstetrician could sometimes become a horsefly which may sting the other, in other words, stimulate and provoke them to give voice to their ideas, whether right or wrong. The consequence is that in the ensuing dialogue, ideas can be developed in a more mature form.

Every idea can be the source of a new life or a more enhanced life. Life, in general, becomes a life in evolution, today fertilizes the tomorrow that has not yet arrived and we can, perhaps, avoid so many disasters that we commonly see, many due to the haste to translate thoughts into actions. Thoughts that were still half-baked, but the oven door was opened too fast or too violently. This is perhaps due to the need to react to certain adverse situations instead of taking time to respond, and so, misunderstandings are born that risk degenerating into disasters. At the level of the sixth chakra, that of the third eye, the listener can instead have a more systemic view. They can see how their interlocutor's choices will affect the present context as well as future generations. They can see them as someone in continuous evolution towards greater wisdom, intervening, if necessary, to offer some suggestions to facilitate this.

Again, at the level of the sixth chakra, the listener can visualize the interlocutor as a kind of antenna through which the messages of the universe are conveyed. Sometimes, the reception is clean and, in this case, the person acts consistently and with satisfaction, but sometimes, the reception could be distorted and the person acts inconsistently, ill at ease and full of contradictions. Having this awareness allows us to intervene with more generous support in a dialogue with our interlocutor.

Finally, at the level of the seventh chakra, known in Sanskrit as *sahasrara*, meaning the sense of union with everything, the listener will be led to imagine that the universe is being reflected in each of the two people. This is a vision that allows us to recognize, welcome and give greater value to the other despite the obvious differences that exist. It is a kind of listening that really allows us to aim for a universe where everyone will be free to discover their hidden genius, their divinity and to convey this energy to others.

A good listener could be described as a person who creates the space within themselves in which all these elements can develop while listening. The reader who wants to make them part of their own repertoire can choose some element on which to start focusing in a future listening session and gradually add some other elements.

14   US AND THEM

The age of nations has passed. Now unless we wish to perish we must shake off our old prejudices and build the Earth.

—*Teilhard de Chardin*

When we think about culture, what comes to mind is the unique way in which a group of people or a population consistently behaves, thinks and gives importance to life events. This defines a mindset, *forma mentis,* inherited and then transmitted from generation to generation. Though subject to mutation over time, culture is what gives a group stability, what brings a sense of belonging, a need that has always been fundamental for the survival of human beings.

The roots of a culture are an example of what the well-known psychoanalyst Carl Jung called the collective unconscious. We do not know from where we learned certain ways of behaving which we hardly ever question but take for granted as right. An example is the way of greeting people, which is typical of a particular country. Another is that seen at sporting events involving different nations when, sometimes, we have absolutely no hesitation in cheering for our national hero even if we are not particularly interested in that sport. A person who does not conform in such ways would feel or may be made to feel like a fish out of water. This cultural imprinting is sometimes noticed abroad when we succeed in identifying one of our compatriots merely by the way in which they move and act, even before they utter a word.

If culture is what unites people, a sort of matrix, a mould for behaving in certain ways, it is also a way of flattening, sometimes, trying to erase one's individuality, levelling out idiosyncrasies, those aspects that characterize each individual. It is a process whose nucleus can be noticed when parents begin to impose good manners on children, partly because they may become good citizens and partly not to make the adult look bad. Children become metaphorically transformed, according to Joseph Campbell's *Reflections on the Art of Living*, 1991, into camels, animals that carry weights, in this case, the burden of traditions, which must be maintained and cannot be refused. This phase of being subject to rules and regulations is necessary to prevent generating a society where anarchy rules. But the exasperation of these norms leads to not valuing the individual and goes towards creating an almost unique mould that serves to standardize all people, thereby eliminating anomalies, those little things that make us different from each other.

And so, we begin to form the group of us. At the same time, the group of them is also formed, and they are different from us. Within each of these factions, much is generalized and we see only the forest and not the trees. We say, for example, that we act in certain ways while they, without distinction, act in different, even opposite, ways. And this is the moment in which we not only differentiate between the two groups, but begin to dissociate ourselves from the other. Our comparisons are not only descriptive, but they conceal a subtle judgment. We do not consider ourselves similar to them, we will never dream of doing as they do, and we come to think or even say that we do things in the right way while they are the ones who make mistakes. We say things like men are rational, women are not thinking beings. Such an attitude easily degenerates into superiority or inferiority.

This sense of us and them is further amplified by using language mindlessly, we are used to talking about us and them without realizing the subterranean process that is being generated. We tranquilly talk about our family, our friends, our workplaces not realizing that these distinctions, on the one hand, serve to give some order by dividing into affinity groups, while on the other hand, can give rise to the formation of clans and sects.

We know how harmful this habit is when, for example, because of a theft committed by a person of a different ethnicity from our own, we label that whole ethnic group as thieves. Or being so attached to our sports team, we feel a great sense of belonging, so much so that we sometimes dress in the same colours as the players to further promote this sense of association. We criticize the opposing team, even if they are stronger, attributing qualities that serve only to denigrate them. In all these situations, it would seem that there is an imaginary wall between the two parts. It is a wall that is erected in the hope of keeping our perceptions and assessments sanitized and clean.

Throughout human experience, perhaps inherited from the animal world, when a person feels that they are superior to another, there may be a desire to conquer the other, to destroy them, to consume them for one's own pleasure or benefit. We lose our critical sense, the ability to discern, we follow orders that are issued by the culture to which we belong, we are willing to do anything, even at the risk of our own life, to defend our flag. That piece of cloth that costs so little but takes on an inestimable value when put on a pole to fly in the wind. In addition to the overt degeneration of such attitudes in the form of war, we see this phenomenon also in religion. Everyone believes that theirs is the best, that it is the only one that leads to salvation and people are willing, as history reminds us, to start a war to prove it.

This attitude of the herd, lumping all together under one label, generalizing and deleting all differences, is what Hitler was able to exploit to carry out his ethnic cleansing. Even those sports fanatics, who have an excess of zeal, may commit equally horrible acts. It is as if they were motivated by a higher order to act in that way and they have no choice but to obey. If everyone should decide on their own that we will no longer be an 'us', then that sense of belonging, which is so important for survival, will be missing. We feel moved by the vibrations of the group, of the flock or clan, and we no longer feel responsible for our choices and actions.

All because we have generalized, creating a schism, a rift between us and them. Although this may not lead to extermination, as in past times, we must be careful because the risk of tyranny is always lurking when we consider ourselves different from others. The next stage is to feel superior. This seems to entitle us to want to iron out or even destroy any form of diversity. And unfortunately, we can experience a certain pleasure in doing harm to those who are different from us.

If we want to overcome these limits, we will remember to differentiate between the individual and the group to which they belong, avoiding lumping all together. When we speak badly, for example, of a category of professionals, we will look more carefully at the individuals that make up the category. We will find that they are not all alike and it is very probable that many of our generalizations will disappear.

We can also recover some of the ground that was lost in the generalization by using language more appropriately which, as we know, will be able to influence our thinking in a more useful way. For example, referring to different cultures and their customs, we can say, 'The people I met in a certain country act in such and such ways.' We can make this even more precise by bearing in mind that the people of that particular country are different from one another, but for now, just for the convenience of language, it is appropriate to forget the differences and the uniqueness of each one so that we can focus on the phrase we want to say. The phrase would become, even if somewhat long and maybe a little unwieldly, 'Despite being a population of extremely different people in stature and ways of speaking, with respect to what I was accustomed to, some of the people I met, in certain situations, tend to abandon their cutlery and eat with their hands.' It is a way of commenting on a costume without judging it.

We are reminded that the Dalai Lama says that when he sees another human being, he sees the same human face and, so, immediately recognizes that they are a brother or a sister. And he says, 'Whether you know that person or not, you can always smile and say hello.'

And as the Pink Floyd sang in their wonderful song 'Us and Them,' after all, we're only ordinary men.

15 ONENESS

The truth is one, the sages call it by different names.

—*Rig Veda Samhita*

The sixth astronaut to set foot on the moon, Edgar Mitchell, in 1971, said he felt an extraordinary connection between the molecules of his body and those of his spaceship and that the world he had left and the one he was returning to had been made in the same oven as the ancient generation of stars like those around us. While for many, this can be an intellectual reflection that comes after a profound meditation, for the astronaut, who sees the planet from above and does not distinguish lines of political divisions between countries, the perception of a connection is immediate, almost natural.

Even the great German philosopher, Arthur Schopenhauer spoke of the innate awareness that we are really one. This is an awareness that, in moments of great difficulty, emerges spontaneously, a glimpse into a greater truth. James Joyce, in his work *Ulysses,* wrote that Stephen Dedalus had asked himself the question if, seeing a stranger who risked drowning, he would be able to forget the instinct of self-protection and jump to save him. It is a question to which firefighters are called daily to answer. In the words of Joseph Campbell, survival is only the second law of life. The first is that we are all one.

There are still populations who live according to this belief. Native Americans feel that when someone dies, it is like if a part of each of us goes away. Maybe, it is something that we commonly experience especially with close friends or even with our pets. We feel a great sadness when someone leaves us, even if it was a companion on all fours and we may find ourselves sometimes in the grip of emotions and tears. It is not that this does not happen when one of our family dies, only that, in this case, it is almost a foregone conclusion. Particularly in the case of pets, the experience is still relatively new as the animal once lived outside the home and was not perceived as family member.

It is alleged that Chief Seattle[5], the Suquamish chief whose name was adopted for the city in the United States, said in what is commonly known as Chief Seattle's Letter of 1854:

> Whatever befalls the earth befalls the sons of the earth. Every part of this earth is sacred to my people. Every shining pine needle shining, every sandy shore, every mist in the dark woods, every clearing and the humming insect are holy in the memory and experience of my people. We are part of the earth and it is part of us. The perfumed flowers are our sisters, the deer, the horse and the great eagle, these are our brothers. Each ghostly reflection in the clear waters of the lakes tells of events and memories in the life of my people. The murmur of the waters is the voice of my father's father, the rivers are our brothers, they carry our canoes and have fed our children.
>
> Remember that the air is precious to us, that the air shares its spirit with all the life it supports. The wind

---

[5] Eli Gifford, *The Many Speeches of Chief Seattle (Seathl): The Manipulation of the Record on Behalf of Religious Political and Environmental Causes* (Scotts Valley, CA: Createspace Independent Publishing Platform, 2015), 38–9. ISBN 978-1-5187-4949-0.

that gave our grandfather his first breath also receives his last sigh. We know this, the earth does not belong to man. Man belongs to the earth. All things are connected like the blood that unites us all. Man has not woven the web of life, he is just a thread in it. Whatever he does to life, he does also to himself.

We love this land like a newborn loves its mother's heartbeat.

There are many wisdom traditions that speak of oneness. According to the Christians, we descend from a supreme being with whom we would like to be reunited after death. The Kabbalist tradition speaks of a source of light that became fragmented, giving rise to individual lives, all of which are aiming at returning to the source from which they derived. The Buddhists, in addition to emphasizing the interconnection between all forms of life and how each influences the other, also speak of reincarnation, a concept that invites us to see ourselves replicated in other sentient beings. In the Ubuntu culture in Africa, the greeting is not, 'How are you,' but 'How are we,' because the condition of one is reflected in the other. Even the naturalist traditions attribute intelligence to vegetable life, for example, to plants, and speak about how they also communicate with us human beings. It is interesting to ask whether walking in a forest and touching a leaf of a plant, is it we or is it the plant that is initiating the movement? In this sense, we can no longer speak of the mind only as something that resides within us but something that exists in our interaction with the environment. All this leads us to what the philosopher Lévy-Bruhl called a participation mystique, something that goes beyond the ratio-nality with which we try to explain the universe.

Even science, through the discovery of the big bang, seems to confirm the sense of a whole from which we were born and from which we then evolved. Perhaps, it is the same one in which, at the end of our life, we will return whether six feet under, in fire, in water or in a form that we do not yet know and that we will never know when, in about 5 billion years when the sun will no longer exist.

The sense of one is also an attempt to go beyond the duality that keeps us apart. Duality is what allows us to keep various opposites in place, for example, light and dark, good and evil. One of the most important dualities is the I and the not-I. If this distinction were not there, we would have great difficulty in having a sense of our identity, of enjoying a certain independence and autonomy and growing according to our own design. It is a duality that we begin to be aware of early in life, when we begin to realize that we are different from our mother, of which we were part until recently and we realize, growing up, or we are taught, that there are differences, one of which is ethnicity, which creates even more difficulties.

When we grow up, we widen these differences when we meet someone different from us, we want to know who this strange being is, where they come from, what their guiding principles are, if we can trust them or if we should suspect them.

Albert Einstein reminds us,

> A human being is part of a whole, what we call universe, something limited in time and space. He experiences himself, his thoughts, his feelings as if they were separated from the rest—a kind of optical delusion of his consciousness. This delusion becomes a kind of prison for us, limiting us to our personal aspirations and affection for a few persons nearest to us.

It is an exhortation to free ourselves from the prison of us and them, to expand our understanding and compassion to the circle not only of the group of family and close friends, but to recognize the wider family to which we belong.

This is a family made up not only of human beings, but of all sentient beings and of all nature itself. It is not an invitation to be a vegetarian, but certainly to have a special regard for all forms of life, while recognizing that according to the law of survival, life consumes life. The hunters of old, when life depended on this activity, knew that what they hunted belonged to the same species, and this was one of the reasons for the ritual of dressing up like the animal they wanted to hunt. And with great respect and gratitude, having consumed all the parts of the animal that could be used, they buried the carcass usually with a bone in its mouth in the hope that in the next season the animal would still be available to sacrifice itself for the sake of the tribe.

But returning to the experience of the astronaut, and thanks to the technologies which, in the past, were just phantasies, we can, today, appreciate how everything is inseparably connected with all the rest. How we also connect with celestial bodies and how, even confirmed by our language, some of our states and moods as well as the tides are somehow influenced by the lunar phases. The holistic doctor Deepak Chopra says that we are the eyes of the universe that is looking at itself from different points of view.

The thought that we are all one may not create world peace, since we can only make sense of the concept of peace if its opposite, that of war, also exists. We can, however, aim for a more harmonious society, knowing that there will always be disharmony and conflicts. But as usual, the time to prepare ourselves is when we are relatively at peace, when strong conflicts are not lurking on the horizon that would risk making us lose our balance, a possibility that is increasingly becoming the order of the day, largely due to growing globalization and migration of populations. Even in the midst of these disturbances, we can still find a moment of calmness to reflect on our basic commonality.

With a little training, this thought could be even more present, preventing us from committing acts of unnecessary violence.

16   DIVERSITY

For the gods all is good and just, but for man certain things are right and others are not.

—*Heraclitus*

Almost all forms of life have their origin, according to biology, in a single cell which, in a process called mitosis, splits into two, then into four. We find this concept of a single unit also in mythology, for example, Adam contained Eve, who was born of his own rib. In the same way, the foetus is contained in a symbiotic relationship with the mother. Life in the womb, in the amniotic fluid, is usually exceptionally idyllic, fed by the mother, who contains the embryo. The mother feels a sense of oneness, which means that she is often not even aware of another presence within, except in moments when she notices, moments in which she may display a marked sense of protection. Then comes the separation, the moment of birth and gradually each one begins to feel the presence of the other, which they can also see through their own eyes, thus, beginning to realize that they are different. Where there was one, now there are two. Birth is the moment when duality begins to have a real meaning.

Duality, generally, refers to opposites, some examples of which are male and female, father and mother, yin and yang, the sun and the moon, day and night, light and shadow, past and future, conscious and unconscious, Jesus and Judas, and in mythology, Demeter and her daughter Persephone. We see that it is a constant that accompanies us until death and favours the creation of order in our mind, comfortably dividing things into two categories, black and white. When we subdivide, we inevitably tend to add the criteria of judgment, good and not good, right and wrong, important and not important. This operation is appreciable when it facilitates us, but less so when it hinders us.

We would like everyone to be a little more like us, that is, in our image and likeness, even if not an exact copy. This would give us a sense that we are on the right path and that our choices are the right ones. In this way, we will create the illusion of living a dignified life and of gathering awards that we hope, in the end, will be to our advantage. But we also know, at a level that is over and above our rational sphere, that we are not able to live without diversity. We can't even begin to imagine how disturbing it would be, if all the people on earth had our exact same face, if they were all dressed exactly like us, had our identical character and were all males or all females, or if in the world we know today, there was no longer the distinction between day and night.

One of the categories that lends itself to particular attention is that of good and evil. We would all like to live on the side of the good, or what we believe is good and this, sometimes, prevents us from recognizing two things. The first is that the opposite of good, evil, exists even though we prefer not to see it. We are so attracted by the candid and white sense of good that we forget that we also have feet that touch the earth. We are not only illuminated by the spirit that raises us, but we also have parts that tend to pull us down. This is the shadow side that we all own, widely portrayed by the dark side of force in the series of *Star Wars* films. The shadow side is the domain of Dionysius, who is underground but always present, and contrasts with Apollo. It is the part we ignore because it is uncomfortable. When we see it in others and we accuse them of behaving in an unworthy manner and, consequently, of being unworthy people, it is like a rude reminder and awakening of that unwanted aspect that also resides in us that we prefer not to see but to attribute to others.

The second consideration, another source of problems, is that we believe that our concept is good is right and, consequently, we think we are the only ones or the few people living correctly while all the others are wrong. It is relatively easy that, in these cases, diversity turns into judgement. We judge people based on their dress both metaphorically and, sometimes, literally. Not only are we different from others, we are better than them. From a simple differentiation, we risk passing, often without realizing, to speak of superiority. We confuse the action with who performs the action. We confuse the message with the messenger and instead of negotiating an agreement between the parties, we are bottlenecked in a confrontation in which each is rigidly attached to their own opinion, to their own mental map. We are led to denigrate those who are different and, therefore, as the flipside of the coin, to value our own qualities as the right ones. These are situations that easily lead to tyranny and war, that phenomenon in which people are more willing to die than to change their point of view.

Without diversity there would be no life. Without the opposite sex, there would be no procreation. Evolution itself is based on diversity. The inherent tendency of life itself is to create novelty. The path of life, for unknown reasons, at some point, deviated from how it was previously developing, giving rise to new forms of life and the advancement of the species. The tropical regions, having more diversity, have more species of life than the polar regions. From diversity, in fact, is born not only new life, but more advanced life which is better able to overcome adversity. Limiting diversity, for example, through incest, would lead to the weakening of one's lineage. Our own truth seems to need another truth, to prevent it from becoming rigid, fundamentalist and unable to survive the continual changes in the world.

Even in the field of creativity, diversity is of fundamental importance. Many inventions would not have been realized if it were not because someone thought differently than before. It is well known that in a group of people, those who are noticeably different are more able to cultivate an open, divergent mind and are, sometimes, more rebellious. Many work groups in companies, in order to facilitate creativity which is fundamental to success, are composed of people who differ in terms of cultural extraction, gender and age. In addition, the coexistence of opposing temperaments and attitudes contributes towards creating that sense of generative chaos which leads to what Nietzsche called a dancing star, in other words, innovation.

There are two main reactions to diversity that have been inherited from the first forms of life. They are flight and fight. When we flee, we move away for our protection, and one of the ways to create this is through a kind of indifference, living in a state of perpetual dissociation from reality and its problems, professing that it does not interest us. It is an attitude that could be noted in some ivory towers, reserved only for intellectuals, for example, in some managerial schools where the professors feel untouchable, while what they are teaching does not match reality. Another way of escaping is in the search for an exile that we hope will serve to give us back the sense of separateness and, perhaps, superiority over others. We may find such shelter in consumerism in the world of material things and even indulging in spiritual practices that, again, we hope will bring us closer to an alleged salvation.

The second reaction to diversity is through fight which, as seen earlier, aims to sanitize our uncomfortable aspects or to annihilate those who have a different point of view.

But there is another possibility which can be a blessing. We can go beyond diversity, travel in the midst of the legendary rocks that Jason had to pass through on the journey of the Argonauts. And the recognition that good needs evil to exist and vice versa, that to masticate we need the upper jaw to meet the lower jaw, otherwise we will not be able to feed ourselves. It would be useless and counterproductive to try to remove diversity.

According to Joseph Campbell, it is necessary to open the soul beyond all fear so as to become mature enough to understand how the tragedies of life are included in its majesty. A good start of openness over fear is to cultivate compassion and love. When these factors are present, many problems seem to melt away or seem even never to have existed. It is a matter of not attacking and clinging even more strongly to our mental maps, but to free ourselves from them and be better able to process the various inputs from the world.

It is a question of shifting our attention more within, without having to rush at the opponent outside, that is the object, the person or concept that bothers us and without having to consume ourselves to eradicate it or them. We learn to stop drinking poison in the hope that the other person will die.

It is, therefore, a question of love not only for others, but, in particular, for ourselves.

17   INTERDEPENDENCE

I am because you are.

—*Ubuntu tradition*

Who among us does not remember the exhortation to be independent, a message launched by parents and by educators when they saw us following in the footsteps of someone in such a way that we risked becoming a copy of them? They said this both because of our attitude and because of our way of thinking that seemed as though we had been plagiarized. Clearly, these people were saying this for our own good, they did not want to see us under the influence of someone without our using a minimum of critical sense, that is, without knowing how to choose between what is right and what is wrong. With respect to the condition of dependence when we were children, independence was truly to be desired, a great step forward in our growth. But the narrative didn't have to end there because beyond independence, there is interdependence.

This is the condition to which the poet John Donne refers to in his poem *No Man Is an Island*, 1624, when he says, 'No man is an island entire of itself, every man is a piece of the continent, a part of the main.' And it is also Einstein's reference when he said that human beings tend to experience themselves, their thoughts and their feelings as if they were separated from the rest, what he called a kind of optical delusion of their consciousness. Even in the metaphor of the net of Indra, we find the same concept of interdependence and interconnection. The net is composed of jewels, each of which reflects the other and each, in turn, is reflected in every other jewel. The system is so interdependent that we can never attribute the origin of an event to something or someone specifically, given that the whole system moves in concert. It is a bit like a musical group that plays jazz, in which new forms emerge continuously.

There is a very interesting koan that comes from the Zen tradition. A koan is a sentence or a question that invites the listener not to use only the rational part of their brain to search for a literal interpretation but invites them to a more metaphorical interpretation. An example of a koan is the statement that on this earth, we cannot find even a single grain of sand. What is the meaning of this? An answer can be found at the end of this chapter.

According to a famous school of Santiago, which included certain illustrious people like Maturana and Varela, there is a kind of structural coupling in life. This means that everyone contributes through their actions, influencing others and the sum of all these interactions gives rise to the environment, the culture and the life of people. This process is called autopoiesis, a term which means that the system is continuously being redefined and is reproducing itself from within. This is also the opinion of the famous geneticist Lewontin, who stated that there is no environment which is, in some way, abstract and independent, and as there is no organism without an environment, there is no environment without organisms. Life is, therefore, something that includes all its parts and at the same time transcends it. According to this reasoning, it is the larger whole that gives meaning to each of us.

This is also a distinguishing feature in the Ubuntu tradition, a way of life of the Bantu population in Africa. The basic thought can be summarized in the phrase, 'I am because you are.' The relational field, that is, the relationship that connects oneself with all other people takes on an important meaning. This relational field holds everything together and informs us that it is necessary to go beyond the attention placed on the individual person and to give more attention to how the relationship is influenced through the behaviour of each party. Any intervention to be carried out, whether therapeutic or by way of coaching, is never addressed just to one individual person but to how that person fits and will again be inserted in the complex whole that is called living together. It is said that it is difficult to be a good person in a bad community.

This is far from the individualism that reigns in many parts of the western world, where less importance is given to the community and instead it is the independent individual who is often rewarded and enjoys the greatest privileges. It is what is seen as early as in school, where competition is rewarded, often at the expense of collaboration. The student is forbidden to copy from another, even though copying, assuming that it does not stem from laziness, could be a genuine desire to learn from a companion who knows more and is an effective way to use the resources that are already present in the system. Perhaps we have forgotten that we were all born in company and that we need another to grow. Perhaps we have forgotten that at least part of our brain, the limbic system that governs our emotions, needs interaction with the others to work and to make our learning not just a list of notions, but a set of more integrated concepts to be used with due care and attention.

The whole concept of communication is also closely related to that of interdependence because it is not just a simple linear transmission of information from one person to another. According to Maturana, communication is a coordination of the behaviour of living organisms, and this coordination is determined by the nature of the structural coupling. Communication becomes a sort of dance in which both people move in concert, somehow creating a new shared identity.

Independence, in this way of reasoning, seems to be more of a political concept, not a scientific one. It is what happens when we ignore the context in which the individual lives and of which they are a part. The word 'individual' has its origins in the concept of indivisibility, that is, a whole, and should, perhaps, be revisited. The individual becomes a 'dividable' so as to highlight the connection they have with everyone else. And that's what Einstein meant when, after seeing how his great work gave rise to the atom bomb, he reminded scientists to focus, even in the midst of their formulas and their equations, on the final user, that is, the sentient being.

According to the concept of interdependence, in which the individual emerges from a whole, personhood should, therefore, always be seen against the backdrop of the community to which a person belongs. Everything that the person does could reap benefits or bring damage not only to themselves, but to the whole community. Each of a person's conquests or victories should, therefore, be seen in the light of their effect on its environment. According to the metaphor of the Hero's Journey, to which a chapter is dedicated in this book, it behoves every hero, that is, each and every one of us, to bring home the fruits of their explorations to their ordinary world and interact appropriately with this community for the good of all. Otherwise, the hero would be considered immature, only in search of honour and praise.

It is, however, easy to believe in a self that is separate from the others. After all, when we see barbaric acts of hostility, which are increasingly reported by certain media forever in search of alarming news, we almost instinctively dissociate ourselves from the people who committed such crimes. Perhaps none of us would like to be compared to any of those dictators who, without scruples, exterminated millions or to terrorists who massacred people. So as not to be equated to them, we feel separated from them. We are different from them, and so we erect walls to protect ourselves from the risk of contamination. Not only that but we consider ourselves better than them and, thus, a certain sense of pride is born, which then becomes a source of great contrast and, consequently, of great suffering.

The reflection of Publius Terentius Afer in his comedy *The Self-Tormentor,* 165 BC, *'homo sum, humani nihil a me alienum puto,'* which means, 'I am a human being, nothing that is human is foreign to me,' or to put it plainly, anything concerning another human being or concerning what they do is not foreign to me. Not only that, but it is like if we all have the ability to express any behaviour including those that we condemn in others. The potential is in each of us, the important thing is to keep in mind its effect on others, on the community to which we belong before activating it, adhering to some basic principles of life that may keep us on the right path.

A final consideration concerns the field of microchimerism, an idea which emerged in the 1970s. Scientific findings indicate that some of our cells may have remained in our mother's womb and may, therefore, influence her immune system as well as be transferred to a future yet unborn child. The result is that some people may have cells from family that they have never even seen. We are an ecosystem made of a patchwork of beings that can influence both positively and negatively our health. As Rumi said, we are not a drop in the ocean, we are the whole ocean in one drop.

Given the concept of interdependence, if we find a grain of sand, this grain is connected to many other grains of sand. So, when we hold a grain in our hands, we're indirectly holding the entire world in our hands.

18

SELF-ESTEEM

You are great and the world loves you.

Legend has it that the newly born Buddha took seven steps and in correspondence with each of them, a lotus flower appeared. Raising his finger towards the sky, he declared, 'Worlds above me, worlds below me, there is no one in the world like me.' According to the Zen master, Daisetz Suzuki, this is exactly what a baby's crying wants to communicate and he goes on to say that all babies are Buddha babies.

No doubt, the newborn is the centre of the family world. Able to command attention, they just have to open their mouth and everyone runs to them, to see if all's well and to hear what they have to say. Soon enough, the babies learn how to take advantage of this aspect to have everyone close by. When they then begin to say their first words, the parents are so happy and proud that they encourage them through repetition of the word, perhaps emphasizing the right pronunciation and expanding it into a more complete sentence. This is a phase in which the baby's self-esteem is never questioned and may even border on narcissism and egocentrism. The child, not being able to differentiate themselves from the rest of the world, is absolutely sure that their feelings and points of view will be shared by everyone else.

As the years go by and the novelty begins to fade, children grow but may still think they are the centre of the universe. A good parent, at this point, would like to direct the child towards a more appropriate point of view in accordance with the prevailing social patterns. It so happens that when the child says a word incorrectly, the playful intervention of before, in the form of repetition that included the right version, gives way to correction. In this action of putting the child on the right track, the parent, especially if they are in the company of friends, may feel a little embarrassed. It is almost like if they themselves were wrong, not just the child. To recuperate from this assumed loss of face, the parent may make fun of the situation and in doing so, ends up ridiculing the child also.

Who was previously the centre of the world and was encouraged to feel this way, now has their head bowed and soul kept in check. Joseph Campbell, quoting Nietzsche, calls this the phase of the camel, which must carry the burden of duties, head down and with the most important value being obedience. Dante calls this phase the morning of life, childhood, also characterized by the shame of not knowing all. It is the phase in which the wings are clipped. Before they were spread open so as to fly anywhere especially outside any predetermined scheme. Now what matters is to make the child conform to the rules of society. This is the phase in which parents may begin to dream that the child will follow a certain profession, in some cultures that of the grandfather, especially if the child is the first-born male. It is the phase in which the human being is confined within the rules and duties of society and lives according to the wishes of the adults. A certain decline in their level of self-esteem may be evident.

School, as well, contributes, through its rules, to compress spurious impulses that, according to the teachers, could damage the community. Often, there are rules laid down, not for upholding traditions and keeping the culture alive but to avoid any deviations to which the school staff is not prepared to respond. The result is that the wings of creativity and uniqueness of the individual are folded in favour of uniformity and having everything under control. We go from the necessary dependence in the first phase of life to the dependence induced by the adults who, believing that they have all the right answers, tend to submit others to their power. The power of dependence is noticed when the child, despite having learned that two plus two makes four and that four plus one makes five, cannot assert that two plus three makes five. This can be seen in the classroom when the child looks at the teacher or the adult for confirmation and approval. They do not believe in themselves enough to venture forth in an answer. Their self-esteem, it would seem, has gone down.

This phenomenon is often seen in society. Adults also seek approval, sometimes, in more indirect ways by placing themselves at the centre of attention, for example, by speaking too much or too loudly, dressing in extravagant ways, often appearing on social media, trying to make up for the attention that was originally offered by parents and perhaps denied too quickly. Some adults, on the other hand, sadly maintain a low profile, avoiding any confrontation. If called to act, such a person, even with a history of past successes that should raise their self-esteem, would tend to remember the negative episodes, confirming the image of themselves as a person not up to par. It becomes a downward spiral going lower and lower.

These are situations that could happen to anyone and in which we feel absolutely incapable. We surrender immediately or we struggle, consuming a great deal of energy to get out of them. A more useful solution would be to recover an adequate level of self-esteem. Even more important would be not to wait for these slips but rather to keep our self-esteem at a good level in all circumstances, a condition that seems to be essential for our happiness.

How to recover self-esteem? A good practice is to recall some moments from our past. Most of us have had moments when, even as adults, we have been welcomed, appreciated and loved. In the jungle of our memories, it is sometimes difficult to retrieve these moments but they surely exist for many of us, if not for all of us. With a little patience and perseverance, we can find three or four of these moments, going back over the years, imagining even how we were loved in our mother's womb. These are moments that tend to fill our system with more dopamine, the neurotransmitter that contributes to self-esteem, putting us in a state of more willingness to be open to new challenges, and not to shut down immediately in the face of difficulties and adversity.

In certain traditions, people use talismans, certain objects to which magical powers are attributed and which bring luck. Everyone can create their own talisman, simply by holding a chosen object while remembering and reliving some moments in which they were appreciated or loved. The object could be anything that the person tends to carry in their pocket—a key ring, a pen, a small knife, a pebble, a ring on one's finger or even something new that we may want to take with us. This technique, called anchoring, can also work without an object by associating the memory with a gesture, any typical gesture one may make, for example, rubbing one's chin, fixing one's hair, playing with an earlobe. A phrase can also be associated and repeated aloud, for example, 'I'm great and the world loves me.'

Regarding pleasant memories that sometimes fade away, there is the story of a tribe in oriental Africa in which the date of birth of a child is counted from the first day the mother mentions her desire to have a child. The mother goes to sit alone under a tree and listens until she perceives the song of the child she hopes to conceive. She then returns to her village and teaches this song to her companion, the future father, so that they can sing together as they make love, inviting the child to join them. During gestation, the mother sings this same song to the baby in her womb. Then she teaches it to the older women and midwives of the village, so that the child at the time of birth is received with this song. All the villagers will then learn the song of their new member and sing it to the child, for example, even in moments of crisis, when they fall or get hurt. They sing it in moments of triumph or in the rites of passage and initiations. This song becomes a part of the marriage ceremony and at end of their life, their loved ones gather around the death bed and sing it for the last time.

Who sang our song? How many people have appreciated and loved us? Although we do not know for sure, we can imagine not only our mother, but all those others who witnessed her belly grow.

THE STATE OF FLOW

Everything is under control, not with respect to others, but to ourselves.

Many sportsmen, both professionals and amateurs, experience special moments when, being so absorbed in what they are doing, are not aware of the passage of time. Even those who do not belong to these categories experience similar moments when engaged in something that they really enjoy doing. It does not have to be competitive in nature, it could be something artistic, for example, painting, music or dancing. It could also be something more private, not necessarily to be performed in front of an audience, for example, a walk, the view of a sunset, or something at home, for example, reading a book, cleaning a corner of the house, reading, polishing shoes, cutting the grass and other activities where there is an element of repetition.

One of the qualities that characterizes this state is a sense of absolute inner silence and quietude. There is no excessive tension, the rhythm of breath is regular and the person feels good without necessarily being aware of this state because they are completely absorbed in what they are doing. They are so focused that they lose contact with the outside world and do not notice the time element. They live in the here and now and it is as if they are playing and enjoying every note of a musical piece, without worrying about what the theme of the song is. There are no expectations regarding the outcome of the activity and there is no interference due to memories of past moments, whether good or not so good. There is a total absence of inner dialogue, so there is neither discouragement nor encouragement. It is a state that the psychologist Mihaly Csikszentmihalyi, expert in the areas of happiness and creativity, in his book *Flow*, 1990, calls the state of flow, well-known especially in sports and, sometimes, also called the state of grace.

This great absorption in sports, music, reading or in any activity in which a person is passionate derives largely from the fact that there is continuous feedback. Even surgeons, for example, unlike psychotherapists, through constant monitoring of vital functions, know at all times if they are doing well, and this is one of the reasons why the surgeon would never want to become a therapist. The therapist, for their part, would say exactly the contrary, that is, in their work too there is feedback because the dialogue takes form as a result of their interpretation of the patient's non-verbal communication.

Another aspect that contributes to the flow state is the degree of difficulty of the work. This must be just above the person's ability so as to keep them constantly engaged in the activity. Otherwise they would become demotivated and bored. When engaged, continuous feedback allows for a more marked readiness and reactivity with a greater sense of energy and vitality. There is also the pleasure in finding challenges and opportunities in which they can express themselves fully; searching, for example, for perfection even in seemingly trivial activities, naturally, without becoming obsessive. The tiles of that floor can be polished even more, the grass in that corner of the garden can be levelled just a little bit more. Everything is under control, not so much with respect to others, but in the sense of having a greater degree of confidence in managing one's own performance in the face of the challenges that they may face in the present.

Despite this great inner focus and total absorption in what they are doing, the person feels more intimately connected with the people they are dealing with, even going so far as to become one with all that surrounds them and in a more extended sense, with what extends beyond the limited context.

When a musician is fully absorbed in the piece, they feel connected to something more transcendental, the so-called music of the spheres, and are inspired by the muses. Balinese dancers do not dance for the public but for the deities with whom they feel an even deeper connection during the state of flow of the dance. Chess players feel they are an active part of a strong magnetic field that embraces the universe. Literature also allows us to feel part of a wider community and to identify with the character or characters of the piece.

We can talk about the disappearance of the social mask. This means finding the self through the experience of doing something we like, getting lost by being fully involved in the activity. It is, therefore, a way of letting go of any extreme attachment to the self, in particular, in those cases in which the self has become inflated beyond measure. This is a state that is seen in people who always want to be the centre of attention, people who act so as to be noticed, rewarded and appreciated by others. These are the people who always talk about themselves, what they did and how good they are, without leaving space in which others can have their say. The condition is often associated with arrogance, technically known as being full of oneself or self-centred and could derive from a remarkable inner fragility that was never taken care of.

The opposite of being full of oneself, self-centeredness is the full self or the centred self. This comes from a state of flow, almost ecstatic, that happens when a person is deeply involved in an activity, not just for their own good but, above all, for a collective good. In these cases, as described before, the person feels a part of a larger and more complex design. All the pieces of their mosaic align to emanate a sort of brightness, an energy that can flow more easily to others, inviting them to take part. It is an energy that can be found in charismatic people, for example, in leaders, and when the charisma is authentic, that is, not manipulative, it is an immense joy to be in the company of such people. This is a joy that one can hardly keep to oneself. To witness a magnificent sunset, for example, or be in a special place in nature are experiences that are so great that we cannot but invite someone else to participate, or as in mythology, even tell it to the reeds that may be growing around.

Whoever lives perpetually in such a state can consider themselves blessed, and fortunately, we can all find our own moments of bliss. This is not just a luxury but it becomes extremely useful to know how to recall the state of flow, of well-being and grace before facing a moment that is, presumably, particularly challenging, or even just to start the day off on the right foot. The journey of a thousand miles, said Goethe, begins with the first step, and that first step, which is half of the work, is right under our feet, that is, right here and right now.

One way, a technique for recalling the state of flow or the centred self is as follows. The first step is to get rid of superfluous thoughts that could weigh down our mental condition. We can facilitate this by shaking our body as if we wanted to shake off what does not belong to us, accumulated things, for example, ballast, unpleasant memories, worries and expectations. Followed by two or three breaths, we can begin to feel or imagine a connection, an alignment inside our body.

The following technique can be facilitated with the support of another person, a coach who may invite us to follow these instructions. It starts with identifying a moment in which we found ourselves in the state of flow and begin to relive it as if it were present here and now. One way to facilitate this is to focus more acutely on certain elements of the situation, for example, what was around, which were the sounds and sensations. This process helps to intensify the experience, to be back fully into the experience and to bring the feelings of well-being into the present. Continuing breathing rhythmically, we can give ourselves permission to enjoy this moment fully, although for some it might seem rather strange to enjoy something that is only virtually present. It is, however, something we do every time a pleasant memory comes to visit us. The difference is that this time it is we who are going to visit the moment. After all, the first step is always right under our feet.

While continuing to enjoy the moment, we can associate a keyword, which can be pronounced whenever we want to recall the state of flow.

Being in the state of flow is a condition that feeds itself. The more we experience it, the more we find ourselves in this state and the easier it is to access it. It is not a bad idea to have it as a companion during the entire day. And the resulting good mood can positively influence interpersonal relationships. It makes us more amiable and contributes to greater well-being in the world.

JUST BE YOURSELF

The river flows day and night, without end.

—*Confucius*

When we are told to be ourselves, usually the perception of the person who says it is that we are somehow not behaving authentically, we are not really ourselves, or that we have been plagiarized by someone. Our behaviour, in those moments, surprises the person we are speaking to, they struggle to recognize us and might think they are relating to a stranger. A typical example is the youngster who goes away from home, for work or for study, and on returning, brings with them attitudes, ways of speaking and doing which they assimilated during this period. Those who remained at home could be confused because they were expecting to find the same person as before. Or worse, they might object to what the young one is expressing because it is in contrast with the education received at home.

In a certain sense, those who express the exhortation 'just be yourself' could be disturbed by the attitude of the other. On the one hand, we always want novelty, otherwise life would be boring, while on the other hand, we want things to remain constant, because this way, they will still be recognizable, not too foreign. We want our cardinal points to remain as they always have been. Although we can be fascinated by some changes, we always need to find solid ground under our feet and to know that we are relating to the same person as before. This is a fundamental human condition, one of great uncertainty that creates problems when interacting with others.

Of course, the young one also has their share of responsibility in this scenario. Perhaps, they exaggerated in wanting to demonstrate how able they were in picking up new attitudes. Or maybe, they wanted to brag about new ways and customs, so as to express their autonomy, the ability to manage their own life, abandoning the old standards of the community to which they have just returned. A more attentive consideration of this context would surely have allowed them to introduce the changes more respectfully.

Even in the absence of these considerations, we can see how the self is always changing. Up to what point does the self remains constant and what changes are there, or rather, how is it continually morphing? A very useful concept, at this point, is that change should be understood not as throwing away what one has but as an extension of one's own possibilities, additional ways of perceiving and reasoning that can also coexist with what was there before.

When we talk about the self, we refer to a set of guiding principles, ways of thinking, living and relating to others. This is a work that is always in progress, because the moment it ceases, we are ready to move on to another life. We have learned to do many things, to reason in different ways, and we learned from different people, often absorbing and internalizing some of their attitudes, often without being aware of these changes. It is a phenomenon known as imprinting, adopting the behaviour of another as our own. We may even begin to talk like them when expressing certain concepts they articulated in ways that particularly impressed us. We can also walk like them, in short, live parts of their lives as if they were our own.

When the internalized model is one and only one, we could speak about cloning, that is, not being our true selves. When, on the other hand, the models are more than one, our changes could be less marked and the disorientation of those who observe us more acceptable. In any case, we must keep in mind that we are a work in progress, that we are a combination of all the people with whom we have had a relationship. Every encounter changes the configuration of our brain which, thanks to its plasticity, takes on a new form to include the new input. This process, when stabilized, is called learning. And again, the configuration changes to let in new information in a process that could last until the end of our existence.

Heraclitus, the Greek philosopher who was active around 500 BC, called this *panta rhei*, meaning that change is the only constant of our life. One cannot descend twice into the same river, because the river in which we had set foot yesterday is not the same river as today. Recent research also shows how the image we have of ourselves is not to be considered as something fixed but according to the well-known neuroscientist Ramachandran, 'An entirely transitory internal construct that can be profoundly modified with just a few simple tricks.' We may consider, for example, the professional racing-car driver, how their self-image varies, shifting, for example, between the steering wheel, the pedals and the seat, in the sense that they feel these components of the car not as things separate from them, but as parts of themselves, extensions of themselves.

The self becomes that shell which, according to Ramachandran, we created temporarily to pass on our genes to our offspring. Our identity, the self, is something in continuous change. While maintaining our name throughout our life, our body changes, it is renewed every year by 98per cent. Can we say that we are the same person as before? If we buy a car and during the course of the next 20 years, we change all the parts inside, leaving unchanged only the body, can we say that the car is the same as that of 20 years before? What is the aspect that must remain unchanged in these contexts, both for the human being and for the car, so we can say that it is the same person or the same car?

Perhaps, it is what the poet Stanley Kunitz calls the principle of being, that road from which, according to him, we struggle not to stray. Or what William Stafford calls the thread that doesn't change between all things that change. This is a phenomenon that can be seen among people who come from a situation of poverty, which defined who they were, that is, theirs was the identity of the poor and, suddenly, they win large sums of money in the lottery. Even if they may change their lifestyle as far as possessions are concerned, they manage to squander the money almost as if to confirm the thesis of their identity of origin, that of poverty. It seems as if they must remain or return as such. Their ascent to richness lasts no more than a couple of years, only to revert to their previous condition, if not even worse.

The thread that does not change between things, that principle of being, is what makes us recognizable in the midst of continuous changes. We are no longer the ones who scream when we are hungry or when the diapers are wet, although, sometimes, we still scream when we should instead of thinking. Someone, maybe, still wants to see us nostalgically as we were in the past, so much so that when they meet us, they greet us by saying that we have not changed at all. But we have certainly grown in so many ways, we are able to manage more complexities of life, something we didn't know how to do once. The thread that does not change, that is, being oneself, refers to some of our values, our guiding principles. For example, our respect for other sentient beings, the continuous search for truth, living in harmony with the world could be the principles of being, those cornerstones that allow us still to be recognized.

There is the saying, translated from Latin, that a wolf may change its skin but not its character. We can expand this proverb by saying that this character includes also certain good aspects. Of course, it is easier to direct our attention to the negative aspects, but with more focus, we can see that the self also maintains its positive aspects.

The deep core of the self still lives on.

21 LOVING OURSELVES

Where there is love, there is life.

—M. K. Gandhi

A result of the constant criticism that some of us suffered in our youth is that we are hard on ourselves. We do not like ourselves as we are, our body, sometimes our psyche and we even question our way of being. Diets to lose weight, plastic surgery to hide the signs of age, going to the gym and sometimes jogging to show off a fit body, even some popular training courses that promise miracles are all witnesses to this phenomenon. The common message is that if we do these things, somehow, we will become better people. Because before we were lacking, full of defects. Defects that we seek to cover up with exhibitionism, extravagant clothing, a flashy car, or trying to lash out into pseudo-academic speeches, perhaps, to amaze the listeners. The latter is a rampant phenomenon today, thanks to social media that allows us to show off more and more. Even with a trivial expense of time, anyone can write, deceiving themselves of being a poet or an inspiration for others. Social media also allows another type of exhibitionism, that relating to personal events experienced, such as travel and restaurants. This causes, according to statistics, about 30 per cent of readers to suffer from a form of envy towards those who appear on these media.

Parents also contribute to living non-authentically, a little distant from ourselves when they seem to manage the lives of their children, who are forced to do a myriad of activities after school, always being obliged to satisfy the desires of adults. This could contribute to preventing them from gaining autonomy and may help increase the sense of not being up to the situation. To avoid the risk of low self-esteem, some modern parents resort to ways of over-praising their children. Maybe, unknowingly equating them with domestic pets, for whom modern techniques of training advise to ignore misconduct but to praise, even exaggeratedly, what they do right. Some parents of children of the generation of the new millennium, that is, those born in the early 1990s, tended to pour rivers of praise even when the actions were part of a child's normal growth. The child who eats everything that was in the plate becomes the object of praise but with the risk that, later in life, they get used to wanting to receive it continuously. Recognition and love are generated on the outside; so, loving oneself is reduced to just empty words that have no real meaning. This internal emptiness, the fragmented self within, can easily lead to narcissism, our thinking that we are better than others, giving birth to the inability to tolerate mistakes, both our own and those of others.

A reflection for those who want to start loving themselves again is to think that even in our imperfection we are not lacking; we are just a work in progress. Instead of condemning our condition of life, we can embrace it, clearly with the intention of improving, without affecting the deeper sense of who we are. We can throw away what we consider inadequate without throwing away the baby with the dirty water. The following excerpt is a slight adaptation from *Meditations of Virginia Satir*, 1991, by Satir, famous in the field of family therapy and is an inspiration to continue along this path. It is a piece to be read slowly and in a meditative state, savouring every single word. Reading it aloud can be a great way to internalize it even better.

I am Me. In all the world, there is no one else exactly like me. Everything that comes out of me is authentically mine, because I alone chose it.

I am Me in all my parts: my body and all that it does; my mind, my thoughts and my ideas; my eyes and the things they see, my feelings whatever they be: anger, joy, frustration, love, delusion, excitement, my mouth and all the words that come out of it, polite, sweet or unkind, correct or incorrect, my voice, high or low, and all my actions, whether they be to others or myself.

I am Me in my fantasies, my dreams, my hopes, my fears. I am Me in my triumphs and successes, all my failures and mistakes. Because I am Me in all my parts, I can become intimately acquainted with me. By so doing, I can love me and be friendly with myself in all my parts. I can orient myself and work towards my best interests.

I know there are aspects about myself that puzzle me, and other aspects that I do not know -- but as long as I am friendly and loving to myself, I can courageously and hopefully look for solutions to the puzzles and ways to find out more about me. However, I look and sound, whatever I say and do, and whatever I think and feel at a given moment in time is authentically me.

If later some parts of how I looked, sounded, thought, and felt turn out to be unfitting, I can discard that which is unfitting, keep the rest, and invent something new for that which I discarded.

I can see, hear, feel, think, say, and do. I have the tools to survive, to be close to others, to be productive, and to make sense and order out of the world of people and things outside of me.

I own me, and therefore, I can engineer me.

I am me, and I am Okay.[6]

This piece can be read in front of the mirror, looking intimately inside ourselves. Usually, we tend to stand in front of the mirror while we are thinking of something else, or we are still too sleepy to realize that there is a human being present. By spending a few moments longer, even just a minute, reading the piece and concluding with, 'I like myself because ...,' referring to who we are rather than what we do in life, could bring great benefits to love for ourselves.

Love for ourselves can also be nurtured by remembering someone who loved us unconditionally. This means without having expectations, like if you really love me, you will know how to read my mind. It also means being free from blackmail by people or parents, who go to extreme sacrifices in life hoping to get thanks and appreciation from their children. The most appropriate relationship is that of grandparents. They have the task of carrying forward certain universal values, one of which is love, and many kids and even adults tend to remember grandparents as the people that gave love without wanting anything in return. Simply reliving the caress or the sweet words of a grandfather or a grandmother leads to a release of chemicals in the brain, including serotonin, that makes us feel good about ourselves.

A very important consideration in this regard is generosity. The greatest joy comes when we can be altruistic and contribute

---

[6] Virginia Satir, *Meditations of Virginia Satir: Peace within, Peace between, Peace among* (Palo Alto, CA: Science and Behavior Books, 1991).

to the good of others. This should be done in a disinterested way, again, without expecting something in return. There are traditions in which to give a gift is a sign of power, when it is known at the outset that the recipient does not have the means to reciprocate. In other traditions, giving is a gesture of love, a promise that a relationship can continue to delight both parties for a long time. The more you give, the more you receive, one would say. According to an ancient Chinese maxim, when you give a flower, some of its perfume remains in your hands.

A curious anecdote about generosity concerns Gandhi who, one day, lost a slipper while getting on a train. All of a sudden, the train left; so Gandhi could not recover the lost slipper. Without a moment's hesitation, he threw the other slipper onto the tracks saying that, in this way, whoever will find the slipper would not have only one but a pair to be able to use.

Lastly, there are people who are universally recognized as emblems of love, for what they are capable of giving. Two of these are the Dalai Lama and Mother Teresa. Just imagining the loving touch they could give us, if they were present, can put us back on the track of loving ourselves.

ECOLOGY

We are all, from the first to the last, parts of the web of life.

Ecology—which, from its Greek etymology, literally refers to the dwelling or to the family, the basic unit of society—originally denoted the relationship between an organism and the world in which it lives. Today, although it is used, above all, as a warning not to exploit and disfigure nature, its meaning extends far beyond, going on to include the interconnections between all parts of a system. In a family, for example, it is easy to understand how all the components are connected to one other, such that an action performed by one member reflects on the whole family for better or for worse. Even in a corporate organization, a similar phenomenon can be observed. Any action made in one part of the whole will, sooner or later, affect the other parts. Even in a mechanical complex, for example, a modern car, largely managed by electronics, a malfunction in one area can compromise the performance of the whole. The concept of ecology was synthesized by Edward Lorenz, in 1963, in the butterfly effect, which says a butterfly flapping its wings in Beijing could affect the climate thousands of kilometres away, after some time.

When we take into account the concept of ecology and the butterfly effect, we open ourselves to a world in which cause and effect are not always immediately predictable. One of the first areas where this can be seen is the field of meteorology. The weather forecast is necessarily short term and, today, is also expressed as a percentage of probability. This is due to the so many variables that participate and contribute to making the system even more complex, non-linear, in other words, chaotic. So much so that the science of complexity speaks of strange attractors, elements that are repeated over and over, apparently randomly, that attract the system towards its destination.

The concept of ecology invites us to remain open-minded and receptive, to appreciate more the asking of questions than the giving of answers. It invites us to live in uncertainty, since we cannot perceive all the variables between an input and the effect we want it to produce. For some, this way of living can be destabilizing, but once accepted, it becomes a source of great creativity because we realize we have so many more choices and possibilities.

According to the concept of ecology, it is not to be taken for granted that an improvement in a limited area will necessarily lead to an overall greater good. Someone or some other party could be affected negatively. Returning to the world of work, a company, thinking of generating more profits, could be induced to increase sales. This will take a greater toll on the production which, if not sufficiently prepared to meet the new need for more goods, will have to rush to produce with the risk of compromising quality. Customers could find themselves dissatisfied and, in the long run, the company may see its profits fall.

Even areas that are less immediately connected will suffer. The company will have to take into account how the human climate will be affected when the workload increases. If not adequately foreseen, the workers could find themselves having to spend longer hours with the risk of greater tiredness, nervousness and possibly more stress, again, compromising the quality of its production. The butterfly that flapped its wings in wanting to increase sales could create a hurricane in the rest of the company, if some considerations are not taken into account before acting.

The butterfly effect also applies to interpersonal relationships. In a couple, for example, both parties will have to take into account how their presence is influencing the whole. If one is angry, they will have to consider how this will affect the other person and, consequently, the relationship. If the other is not ready to accept and manage this emotional condition, it could trigger a negative spiral in which the person who was angry falls into an even worse state, contaminating even more the relationship of the couple. If the person had given some more thought before expressing themselves, they could have adjusted their words so as to maintain a minimum of sanity and balance in the system. The same reasoning also applies to those who express a euphoric state when the other is not ready to accept it.

The ecological approach takes into account the following factors. The first is space. When we are about to make a decision, we need to evaluate the consequences not only for ourselves, but the effect on other people who may be involved, both near and far. If a person wants to go on vacation to a certain place but their partner disagrees, some incomprehension will be inevitable. This is also true in the choices that seem to concern only one individual. Since no one lives in complete isolation, a person who does not care enough about their health, claiming that it is not a problem, could create concerns for other members of the family. A person who dresses in a certain way to satisfy their own taste should reflect if they will be received with admiration, disdain or envy when meeting other people. The choice of an entrepreneur to discharge waste into rivers could be very convenient for them, but the effect of this action is measured in terms of how many other people will be involved where that polluted river passes. Any decision of a political nature will clearly affect many people. A xenophobic thought that translates into actions, as history teaches us, could have a huge impact on a considerable part of the world.

The second aspect is time. Any decision or action has consequences that are immediate but will also reveal themselves in the future and would not be immediately recognizable without an in-depth reflection. The effects, sometimes, take a certain amount of time to manifest themselves. In addition to the classic example of the ozone hole, which was formed over time, largely due to the use of certain chemical substances, it is important to take into account what we consume, in terms both of food and drugs. Dysfunctions, such as side effects, appear over time. This reasoning also concerns any action whose effects could involve other people, that is, according to the previous paragraph, anything we do. Any decision to be taken is not just about the present, but the benefit it will bring to the future generations must be considered, that is the legacy to be left to them as a guarantee for their evolution.

The effects in space and time can be seen, for example, when an oil tanker loses its load or discharges it into the sea, creating damage measured not only in the immediate vicinity of the disaster, but in the length of time during which the consequences could last.

An area where ecology plays an important role is tourism, which has now become more affordable to many people all over the globe. Even the most remote countries are affected by waves of tourists, many of whom do not care about the consequence of their presence on others. If, on the one hand, this could lead to an improvement in the standard of living in some areas of the world, those so-called depressed areas, on the other hand, certain people lose their endogenous aspects by wanting to emulate the tourists, dress like them, eat fast food, use drugs and alcohol and even buy some goods that are typical of consumerist opulence, for example, villas and flashy cars. Ecology requires that the tourist or visitor leave a light footprint that does not damage the soil where they set foot.

Living the concept of ecology means continuously asking questions. We will never be able to foresee the consequences of our actions in time and space, and this uncertainty is greatly increasing, given the complexity of the context in which we live. Even before we speak, we are invited to reflect, according to Socrates, if what we are going to say is true, necessary and kind. We want to avoid being the kind of person who can sometimes be wrong but never has doubts.

Living the concept of ecology also allows us to get out of the prison of egocentrism, the condition that means not thinking of others, because we believe that our decisions are valid for all. Ecology is, therefore, a way of living with more respect for all that surrounds us, not only for the environment, but also for the physical, mental and spiritual health and well-being of all sentient beings.

Ecology also affects some other aspects that are somehow related to nature. One prime example is eco-feminism. This deals with the condition of the female, who has been the object of exploitation over time, because she is considered in the same way as nature, as Francis Bacon said, to be squeezed and exploited to its limit.

Ecology reminds us, in particular, to deliver a world that is still liveable for the future generations.

It reminds us, before acting, to ask one more question.

WHAT DO YOU WANT TO BE WHEN YOU GROW UP

The future is no longer what it used to be.

—*Arthur C. Clarke*

The time at our disposal, said Steve Jobs in his speech at Stanford in 2005, is limited, therefore, he warned us not to waste it by living someone else's life. He urged us not to remain trapped by dogma, that is, living with the results of other people's thinking, allowing the noise of the opinions of others to drown out our inner voice. This is a kind of wake-up call that invokes us to open our eyes and live our lives. In a similar vein, the message of the well-known sage Lao Tzu, about 2,500 years ago, reminds us that only by giving up the life that we are currently living, can we really become what we could be.

The hidden persuader, to become someone that others want us to become, is still very powerful today. Messages that are apparently well-intentioned, not only from our families, but even in the media, force us to take directions that, if not corresponding to something that is deep within us, can lead to great disappointments. Some parents want their son to become a doctor, thus, nurturing a faint hope that that child will be a kind of saviour for them when they become elderly. It would come as no surprise that there are those who abandon their university studies, those who go to work unhappily and those who buy the lottery ticket in the evanescent hope, in most cases, of finding a better life.

How can we understand which is the most appropriate direction for each of us? How can we realize if we are expecting a fish to learn to climb a wall when such a feat is not in its nature? It is necessary to understand the deeper preferences a person showed or began to manifest as a teenager. For example, did that person seem attracted by numbers and calculations, or by art, by manual skills? Were they motivated by interpersonal relationships, or did they prefer to be alone to meditate and find solutions? Did they like talking in public, singing, or did they prefer listening? Sometimes, the skills are less obvious, for example, did the person prefer order, for example, by arranging their toys or did they prefer chaos, throwing everything up in the air and having fun seeing how the pieces fell, were they more careful to follow the instructions, reading the manual when they were holding a new tool or toy, or did they prefer to find out how it worked as they played or used it.

Each of these trends could indicate a useful direction to take in adulthood, turning it into a profession. It could be said that each of these is a kind of call for one's own journey, a part of the hero's journey, as explained in this book in the chapter 'The Hero's Journey'. It is a call that should we refuse, we would forever be discontent, we would be continually searching for something new to satisfy us, something that would keep eluding us, difficult to find.

When the person takes, instead, the road that could be called theirs, it means that they are following their dream, a sort of pole star, a vision that although sometimes too nebulous to describe, as Walt Disney puts it, will always be what attracts them, what motivates them to go ahead, despite the many difficulties that could be found along the way. This is one of the conditions that allows a person to be more authentic because their words and deeds are aligned with their heart. The person really blooms, becomes fully themselves, and manifests themselves to the world in all their splendour, with great charisma and are able to inspire and elevate anyone with whom they come into contact. It is usually a great pleasure to be in the company of such people, one feels enriched and transported to a higher level of self-realization.

How do we go about becoming like that? Again, it is Steve Jobs who reminds us to have the courage to follow our heart and our intuition because, somehow, they already know what we can really become. Evoking intuition can be done by reconnecting to one's wake-up call, to those activities that a person preferred to do in their youth, while courage can be nurtured in company of an expert, for example, a coach. Even if we did not find the job that perfectly matched our nature, we can all find, in what we currently do, something that recalls those trends demonstrated at an earlier age. Sometimes, such a nucleus, even if small, may be sufficient to find motivation even in a job that risks becoming monotonous or boring.

Another aspect of fundamental importance, which really makes for a more authentic self, is whether what we are doing or the career we want to take is aligned with our values and could benefit humanity. This is because one of our greatest satisfactions is derived from contributing to the welfare of others, even gratis, without expecting anything in return. One of the best ways to find ourselves, said Gandhi, is to lose ourselves in the service of a cause, something that will contribute to a greater good and, ultimately, contribute to a better quality of life.

Once we have identified the area that corresponds to our call, we need to refine it, in other words, to find the tools that will allow us to express ourselves more easily and fully. Fortunately, there is no shortage today of courses and specializations pertaining to any branch one wishes to undertake. But we need to embark on such paths with an attitude of great receptivity, free to explore, to remain open and full of questions, without rushing to find answers that end up switching off creativity and trapping us in dogmas that, in the long run, would only dampen our passion and enthusiasm. It should be borne in mind that the path of improvement should lead to living more fully one's experience, as mentioned before, keeping in mind the human context in which it will be expressed.

And therefore, living it as a mystical participation, according to the philosopher Levy-Bruhl, not only rationally and aimed at a utilitarian scope. Levy-Bruhl was referring to how traditional people managed to conceive any activity as part of a whole, as if every part melted into the others, contributing to make the whole fuller, more complete and harmonious. We could even talk about how even the outside world around us is inhabited by other powers and influences, that some call deities, who contribute to the magic in which we live.

Finally, we need to find an audience that wants to receive our gift. It is said that the meaning of life is to find one's gift, while the purpose of life is to give it away; obviously, to those who are looking for it and are ready to receive it. Even here it takes a certain amount of courage, in addition to the belief that what we are offering will be of great benefit to others. Not always will people accept our gift, sometimes, because they don't realize its value, at other times, because they are engaged in something else. Great discoveries arose not because someone requested them, but because someone had the foresight, the passion and the madness to create something and make it attractive to the public.

At this stage, feedback takes on fundamental importance. It allows for a better calibration of our offer based on the needs and wishes of the public. It is the stage at which we want, however, to be careful not to replicate what others are doing, otherwise the work will soon become boring or stressful because the only motivation would be to eliminate any competitors. Indeed, following one's own path means living in an area of high turbulence, always uncertain, because the road has not yet been traced. All is yet to be explored, which means even making mistakes and starting all over again.

But as long as our offer corresponds to the design of our life and contributes to the well-being of the world, that is, it does not destroy it, but supports it, allows it to evolve, it will be of great interest and utility for a large number of people. This is due to our interconnection with the universe, whatever comes out of it will naturally contribute to enriching and increasing the harmony and charm of this magical world. A world that is a mystery to keep exploring.

And we will also remember to place our trust in our lucky star, our rationality and our planning, despite having important implications which are always limited. Our soul, quoting the poet John O'Donohue, already senses the world that awaits us.

24   ARCHETYPES

A primordial sound of which all other sounds are subtle echoes.

—Ken Wilber

Archetypes, the derivation of which in Greek means primitive models, can be defined as configurations of primary energies found throughout the human species. These were probably inherited, a bit like instinct in animals, and become a sort of 'template', a model for our ways of thinking and behaving. They are the myths that are hidden, encapsulated in every corner of our unconscious being.

These are, according to the Neapolitan philosopher Giambattista Vico, the fantastic universals that are found in all parts of the world and do not depend on the culture to which they belong, as is the case with stereotypes. They are present without any contact between the various people. According to Carl Jung, archetypes belong to the collective unconscious, that primordial soup from which we all emerged and we, therefore, carry these forms of energies inside us. Stereotypes, on the other hand, again, according to Jung, belong to the personal unconscious, which is a constellation of individual experiences as well as the uses and customs of the culture in which the person lives. Archetypal energies are, therefore, innate, dating back to before our birth and are referred to as the pre-personal domain. Not by chance, the incision on the door of Jung's house in Kusnacht, Switzerland, bore the phrase, 'Invoked or not invoked, the Gods are present'.

Archetypes are present in fairy tales and mythology and usually lend themselves to immediate and universal understanding, even if translated into different languages. We notice their presence without necessarily having studied this subject and, often, the word itself evokes something that resonates at an intuitive level within our soul, rather than in the intellect. An example is the figure of the hero, common to many stories and many films, whose meaning needs no explanation. Certain symbols as well, for example, the labyrinth, which can be admired everywhere, and geometric shapes as circle, square and triangle evoke something common to all human beings. They refer to something that resides in our unconscious mind and does not need to be processed by the conscious, rational part. It could be said that archetypes are like seeds, some of which are waiting to sprout and bloom, while others are already flowering and, somehow, direct our modes of existence. The latter are the platform on which our daily life takes place, and one could deduce which archetype is in play by how a person thinks and acts.

A fundamental characteristic of archetypes is that they always have two polarities that coexist, as if they were two sides of the same coin. These could be called the illuminated side and the shadow side. Since one cannot exist without the other, it is not useful to neglect or repress the shadow side, but it is better to recognize how these two opposing energies are at stake, aiming at an appropriate balance so as to live in a state of fullness.

Usually, a person moves within a restricted number of archetypes. This way of proceeding becomes a sort of comfort zone, in which a person feels obliged to act always in the same way in any situation. Some people have a painted smile and always want to be of good humour, optimistic even in the face of difficulties, while someone else may follow a more rational process by way of looking for a solution. There are those who, without thinking twice, act almost on instinct and those who take time to ponder. These are all valid ways, but constantly acting in one and only one way can lead to a certain rigidity, not allowing us to find solutions to overcome certain impasses of life. Usually, when an impasse occurs, it means that another archetype wants to bloom and become part of our way of expressing ourselves in the world. The more acute the discomfort, the more insistent is the force with which the new archetype is calling us to recognize it.

From the infinity of archetypes that exist in nature, the exploration in this book is dedicated to five of the most common, which, according to the authors Moore and Gillette, are the king/queen, the warrior, the magician or alchemist, the lover and the trickster, also known as the jester and the rascal or the divine swindler.

Each of these, when we succeed in accessing them, allows us to express extremely powerful states that enable us to function optimally.

25   THE WARRIOR

The warrior, as the name suggests, is the classic archetype of action. They destroy but not at random and not just for the sake of destroying. They only destroy what they believe should be destroyed in the service of a greater benefit, for example, to protect and maintain one's boundaries, one's integrity or that of a community and, in general, of all humanity. The warrior, therefore, acts for a transpersonal cause, that is, not for reasons related to their ego, their personal desire or to affirm their strength and prowess.

There is a story of a samurai who had to avenge the death of his master, who had been killed in an unfair manner. The samurai, after much searching and after overcoming extreme dangers, sometimes, risking his own life, managed to find the killer. The moment he drew his sword, ready for the attack, his opponent spat in his face. The samurai, at this point, could not do anything but put his sword back in its sheath and leave. When asked why this gesture, he replied that at that moment he was so angry that he would have killed his opponent not for the cause for which he had committed himself, but he would have done so mainly for a personal reason, that is, for the offense that his ego suffered.

One of the features that makes the warrior's job effective is clarity. The warrior, according to author Carlos Castaneda, knows what he wants and how to get it and has the flexibility to adapt to different circumstances or to find the Achilles heel in his opponent, which could be a single person or even a situation. This is the example of Ulysses who faced various dangers while wandering for many years. His return to Ithaca was always clear in his mind, and he succeeded in destroying the pretenders to his throne.

The warrior also has a very high degree of focus and determination. Napoleon felt himself guided towards an end that he did not even know and said that as soon as he reached it, even an atom would have been enough to disintegrate him. But until then, not even all the forces of humanity could have done anything against him. This is also the determination of a professional athlete, so focused towards the finish line and so determined to reach it that they enter an altered state in which their courage is greater than their fear. As Jodorowsky wrote, when one enters deeply in that dimension which they call the dance of reality, the universe dances around the warrior and they find what they were looking for.

The warrior is endowed with great ferocity and aggressiveness, which, as said before, are not manifestations of power but are qualities that are addressed towards a transpersonal cause, that is, for the benefit of the community. The awareness of death is a constant companion, so much so that the warrior lives every day as if it were the last. This allows them to act with great pathos, ability and precision, sometimes, as in the case of Martin Luther King, reaching such a high level as to put even their own life at risk.

The deities, too, have their warrior appearance, for example, they unleash thunder and lightning, or as in the case of the Buddha Manjushri, who uses the sword not to kill but to cut off ignorance. Durga and Kali are the Indian deities that on the one hand create, and on the other destroy, always for a transpersonal cause.

The warrior often has the support of spiritual mentors, for example, a sorcerer or a fairy but, in any case, cannot perform without the support of other archetypes, the absence of which would risk turning the warrior into a fundamentalist. The Indian *Trimurti*, the figure in which the three deities coexist—Brahma the creator, Vishnu the preserver and Shiva the destroyer—is a classic example from the Eastern world.

Even Martin Luther King suggested to enrich the warrior with the lover, using the weapons of love; while Gandhi spoke of sharing truths with love, otherwise both the message and the messenger could be refused. The warrior, consequently, becomes the compassionate or peaceful warrior.

The shadow side of the warrior is the sadist, often seen in wars and especially in guerrilla warfare. These are often people who destroy or kill as a reaction to a personal offense or to show their superiority, trying to substantiate their actions as if they were for a just cause. These are the cases in which the warrior has lost connection to the value of life and the call to a greater purpose.

The masochist is also a shadow side of the warrior. They are the ones who are impotent and let themselves be abused by others or by situations, even deriving a kind of pleasure from this.

THE MAGICIAN/
THE ALCHEMIST

The magician is the archetype that represents knowledge, wisdom and, as the word itself says, magical powers. They know things that others do not know and are able to see below the tip of the iceberg. The magician perceives connections, causes and effects not immediately visible to a common audience, those connections that are the basis of the net of Indra. Indra is one of the divinities of the Indian pantheon and the net is the metaphor that says that every human being is like a jewel that reflects all the other jewels and in which they are in turn reflected. The wisdom of the magician and their ability to perceive allow them to have access to data that is not readily available to everyone, and they, therefore, know how to process it to make decisions with greater clarity. Magically, they succeed, without tricks and deceit, in identifying which buttons to press to convey the right vital energy to solve problems. Even in common parlance, it is said that a magician is the one who is able to find solutions where others struggle. In a more technical and esoteric vein, this is the archetype of the alchemist.

The magician is, particularly, in demand when a crisis arises or in times of transition in life. In these cases, they appear as a shaman, healer, therapist, coach and, in a certain sense, also as a medical doctor. One of their strengths is knowing how to dissociate, taking appropriate distance from the problematic situation that someone may be experiencing, so that they can see it with greater objectivity. In a sense, they are like someone observing a fish swim in an aquarium. The observer, being out of the water, can capture many aspects of the environment in which the fish lives but, of which, it is not aware. This ability of the magician to dissociate can become a limit when taken to extremes. A typical example is the doctor so focused on resolving a problem that they forget that the patient is not a clinical case but a human being.

Even the detective Sherlock Holmes, although a classic example of a brilliant mind, capable of connecting all the dots under the surface, that is, finding solutions that others did not see, was so passionate about his work that, from a human point of view, he became cold and detached. Not to mention the legendary character from the *Star Trek* series, Mr Spock, a native of the planet Vulcan, who lives strictly according to logic, distancing himself from any emotion.

The magician has a great capacity for analysis which is fundamental in some professions, for example, the pure scientist and the mathematician. Their curiosity, in the sense of the search for the truth, leads them to discover the secret powers of the universe. Their calling is then to share these secrets with others, often, in the role of an educator. In addition to using classic teaching approaches, the magician is also an expert in enchantment and storytelling, which will allow the listener to travel inside an experience and find, autonomously, answers that lead not only to solutions to a problem, but, above all, to a transformational change. This is comparable to the alchemical transformation from lead or from mercury to gold, that is, what seemed opaque becomes transparent, understandable and a source of great wealth.

The magician, too, like all archetypes, has a shadow side. In the information age in which we live today, any request for clarification can be satisfied within a few seconds through an internet search engine, merely by typing a few words without even having to formulate a complete question. In addition to the instant gratification that comes from this, it can be noticed that those who manage to get such rapid information seem to take on an air of greater respectability, enjoying a condition of false notional superiority, ready to give explanations and even to dispense advise to others. In this sense, sciolism, which is nothing more than having a collection of data, soon becomes a question of power. This is the magician who has descended into the world of tricks and deceptions, in other words, that of manipulation.

In addition, black magic and the evil eye used to bring misfortune are manifestations of manipulation and power. This is the power to intercede with the divine and spiritual forces of the universe which, originally, were destined for good, for example, in the case of voodoo, one of the world's oldest religions, but were later transformed into a manifestation of power over others.

Any cult could be compared to manipulation and, therefore, to the shadow side of the magician. Even those who use a particular terminology, understandable to a select few, for example, doctors, lawyers, psychologists, sometimes without realizing it, distance themselves from the rest of the population, also involuntarily, showing a certain superiority with respect to normal human beings. For some, it is a way of gaining more credibility, for others, it has become a habitual way of relating to others.

The shadow side of the magician is also present in some teachers, also colloquially called gurus. Through this respectable status, they manage to exert such influence on their students that the result is brainwashing, done either explicitly or subtly.

Another aspect of the shadow side of the magician, on a more passive note is the ingenuous person, the so-called eternal child.

They express themselves by pretending not to know, perhaps, accompanied by an innocent smile. They pretend to be curious and with a face lit up like a child's, they draw attention to themselves. If they are denied this, they manage to create in others the sense of guilt for having attacked the helpless child.

27   THE TRICKSTER

The trickster belongs to the category of the magician, more specifically they are the jester, the rascal, also called the divine swindler. Commonly known as those who practise sleight of hand, those who make objects disappear or make them appear out of nowhere, this is the archetype that refers to whoever mixes up the cards, makes us stumble, especially when we are taking ourselves too seriously. They seem to want to distract us from our journey of exploration but are really allowing us greater growth. By making fun of ourselves, they ingeniously tease even those who are in their company while communicating things of great importance. Their unpredictable way of behaving, of lightening up a situation by not respecting the pre-established values but breaking them up or even toppling them in order to build ones that are more useful to the context, serves to introduce a new range of possibilities when things seem to be stagnating.

The trickster, therefore, opens up several alternatives when the road seems to be only one and when conformism reigns. Their purpose is to break away from traditions, with appropriate lightness, to search for new profound truths. Some of their instruments are satire, jokes and anecdotes that, because of the lightness they bring, allow people to reach much more important and profound reflections than if everything had been done in a serious and arduous way. With this approach, the trickster even manages to direct us to re-examine the values of life and of our own self. In any kind of learning, generally speaking, a good balance between seriousness and lightness allows new notions to enter more easily into our system.

The trickster can be defined as the emblem of uncertainty. But any meeting with them leaves its mark. We may hate them, fear them, but at the same time, we are captivated by their charm and rebellious nature. Their anarchic spirit is honoured in some cultures with masked feast days in the form of the carnival, an event that never ceases to intrigue us, thanks also to the colourful attires and rhythmic sounds. Even on a more day-to-day level, for example, the stage magician, though knowing that they are not really transforming the objects or the people they act on, we struggle to take our eyes off what they are doing because what they are doing seems to be so out of the ordinary. The trickster often ends up being the figure that evokes more sympathy in a story or in a theatrical work, compared to other more common and more normal characters.

One of the uncertainties of the trickster is that we never know whether to trust them, we don't know if behind the mask lies a scoundrel or a hero. The clown is a typical example, a character that brings such instability as to be feared by many people. On the good side, they convey supernatural, almost divine energy. Not by chance, clowns are used in hospitals because their continuous shape shifting makes life richer and less sad. The clown can invite anyone in their company, whether it be the bedridden patient or a relative, to look deeper into themselves, to reconnect with their often-ignored divine aspect. Such an approach allows us to abandon, sometimes, quite forcibly, certain habitual ways of leading life, revelling in the comfort zone and waiting for healing to come from the outside rather than calling upon our inner strength to collaborate.

The trickster, as a deity, can be seen in the example of the legendary snake that tricked Eve to eat the forbidden apple, consequently, robbing humans of their immortality but, at the same time, according to the legend, giving rise to the reproduction of species.

As a deity, the trickster often occurs in native American culture, usually in an exaggerated and absurd form with one part that is body and another that is transcendent, such as Spider Woman or the raven who stole the box containing the sun thereby bringing light into the world. The trickster is found also in cartoons, an example being *Road Runner*. In Europe, it is the figure of a fox, while in India, it is the deity Hanuman, personified by the figure of a monkey, always up to one of his pranks.

The African culture is also full of tricksters. A story that embodies this archetype is that of a conflict when the people see a character wearing a big hat and passing among them. Those on his right side see that he is wearing a red hat, while those on the left see that he is wearing a blue hat. The population, to put an end to the issue, turn to the king, who orders the mysterious person to present himself with the hat that is the source of discord. The character, a trickster no doubt, walks among the people with the king present, who notices that the hat is of two colours, one half red and the other half blue. He, therefore, invites him to turn back so that those who first saw red will now see blue. The king observes that the character, about to reverse the direction of his walk, turns around the hat on his head, so that people continued to see the same colour. When pressed for an explanation of this strange behaviour, he replied that sowing strife, that is, instability and chaos was his occupation.

In the world of cinema, known tricksters are the Marx Brothers, Totò and Charlie Chaplin. In his film *The Great Dictator*, in the midst of comedy, there was a profound message invoking democracy while warning about the dangers that dictatorship could bring.

The shadow side of the trickster regards those who have become unstable, fickle and change continuously because of a lack of conviction and focus. It also concerns those who try to reduce everything to laughter, using irony as a subterfuge, to avoid taking the situation in hands and end up, perhaps, denigrating others. Even children and adults, who constantly disturb, always inventing new strategies for their pranks, belong to this category. Last but not least are those politicians who recycle themselves so as to adapt to the current trends, waving the flag that is most popular or most appropriate for their own purposes.

THE LOVER

This is the archetype of intimacy, tenderness, kindness and, above all, compassion and it is also accompanied by vivacity and passion. It is the world of Eros and Kama, not to mention that of Agape, love for all mankind. The lover is extremely sensitive to the surrounding environment and can grasp its fine nuances by making use of their five senses. They thereby succeed in creating an emotional and empathic bond with the world. They can easily put themselves in the other's shoes, sometimes getting sucked into a relationship without realizing what is happening to them.

The lover appreciates all that surrounds them, that is, all sentient beings and nature itself. They appreciate every morsel of what they eat, every facet of what they are doing, thus, becoming one with everything around them. In particular, they tend to want to unite or to unite better the existing dualities, for example, self and others, elements which, according to many traditions of wisdom, were originally all together in the primordial soup of the universe and which got separated at birth.

The character of the lover allows them to transcend themselves, that is, to go beyond that sort of prison which, according to Einstein, limits us in our personal aspirations and affection for a few close friends. They live their life with selflessness and generosity, not in order to receive praise, not for specific hedonistic reasons to maximize their happiness, but because they feel connected to others and are in the service of humanity. This transcendental connection, in other words, with their divine part is what, according to the poet Emerson, allows us to see the divine grandeur also in 'porters and sweeps'.

Even the sense of sacrifice takes on another meaning compared to the warrior. The lover, through empathy, feels united with the world and may find it relatively easy to do without their kidneys, for example, for the sake of another and, above all, for the good of the extended family of human beings. A case of extreme transcendence, particularly significant and noble, is that of the crucifixion. Jesus abandons his material life for the spiritual one and does so with great joy, going to the cross like a bridegroom to the altar. It is a moment of great ecstasy, going beyond the mundane for a greater good. This is a moment that can be repeated daily, through refinement and elevation of the senses, with the intention not only of doing good, but of being be a vehicle of goodness. When we do good, we may be of support to one or a few individuals; when we are good, we may be assisting all of humanity.

Even in the world of work, in which one of the prime objectives is to make money and beat the competition, a world that is based on strategies, numbers, reasoning and rationality and does not allow any emotion, there is great need for the archetype of lover. The poet Kahlil Gibran speaks of work as love revealed, that is, made visible. He recommends doing what needs to be done with dedication and from the heart, as if the receiver were our loved one who will enjoy the fruits of our work. And he says to extend the breath of our spirit into everything we do. This contributes towards making the workplace more inviting, more motivating and it becomes a place where people can realize their potential, becoming what they really can become.

The artist is another example of the archetype of lover, as they dip their brush into their own soul and then share this gesture with the world through the strokes they draw on their canvas. With their highly developed aesthetic sense, they perceive all life as art and wish to unite with the mystery in each of its manifestations, whether tremendous or fascinating. Their search is that of transcendence through beauty, relationship and sensual experiences. Their response to demons is to seduce them or to convert the experience into something pleasant. The artist, as a lover, is very skilled in the use of intuition and expressing psychic powers.

Their visceral connection with all sentient forms allows them to feel and intuit even the smallest changes. In the *Star Wars* saga, the legendary character Obi Wan, apart from being a Jedi warrior, could feel the disturbances in the force and this was one aspect of his lover archetype.

The lover, too, has their shadow side. An example is addiction, which could be related to food, money, work, clothes or even sex. Such a person may find themselves pulled into such situations, jumping from one instance to another, with a sense of compulsion and restlessness. They will be looking for external solutions, not yet having found the source of love within themselves. There is a continuous illusion that the next experience will be the one that will really satisfy them. This is the Don Juan syndrome that populated many films in the *James Bond* series, in which the protagonist in the last scene was typically shown in bed with one of his female conquests.

Sometimes, it might seem that the lover is expressing a great sense of intimacy when instead it is their extreme need to possess or to be possessed. It is something that can be noticed even in some working contexts in which the boss appears extremely benevolent but, in reality, they want to take possession of their collaborators. The inverse is when an employee is so accommodating because they want to be possessed by the boss, in the hope of being repaid with favours and with more goodness.

Even in the relationship of a couple, there may be the shadow side when one claims they cannot live without the other or relies on the other in a parasitic manner. The shadow side of the lover could be compared to an entanglement, or it may be the femme fatale, a sort of black hole that sucks in everything that comes close. Sentimentalism sweetened with saccharin is also a manifestation of this.

Another manifestation of the shadow side of the lover is impotence. This is the inability to be involved in a situation, remaining emotionally distant from everyone and everything. Such a person never finds anything new in life, there is no freshness in their faces, every physical step they take may seem to be monolithic. Everything seems already seen and already lived and their language becomes arid and bland. The impotent lover is monotonous and, in the long run, risks entering a state of depression.

29   THE KING/QUEEN

The king/queen archetype is the one that restores order in life, allowing us to emerge from the chaos in which we may find ourselves. It refers to the chaos that Picasso depicted in his famous Guernica painting, or in ancient times to what Queen Isis of Egypt had to do, that is, to reconstruct the body of her husband, King Osiris, from the pieces that had been scattered around. And it is also the daily chaos in which we live since we do not know the rules of the game of life. We do not have a user's manual for the brain and due to several current phenomena, such as globalization and the internet, complexity and uncertainty are always on the increase.

The king/queen, metaphorically, receives the laws and rules that serve to stabilize, organize and adjust the system. This is not so much the Solomonic decision of what is right and what is wrong, but it is more a reconciliation of the conflicting dualities that continuously populate our lives. If, for example, we were to ask ourselves the question, 'Who am I', and having got an answer, we were to ask the same question again, this time in the form, 'Who else am I', we will realize that we are made up of multiple aspects, some of which are in stark contrast. We can, for example, be calm and even vigorous, we can love order and also have compartments of life in which chaos reigns, sometimes, we are fierce and, sometimes, lenient, we have a masculine part that dominates in the form of yang energy and a feminine part that contains yin energy. These contrasts can be a source of internal conflict when we do not realize that their presence is part of all human beings. The function of the king or queen is to harmonize the person, recomposing their psyche from any fragmentation and putting it in accord with the rhythms of the universe. This radiates a sense of deep well-being and nourishes calmness in people, even in the alpha male, setting him apart from the aggressive male chimpanzee.

The king/queen facilitates all the other archetypes to transit towards a condition of transcendence, that is, a state in which they are not attached to their ego and their actions are, consequently, directed towards a common good. This includes the warrior with their determination and focus, the magician with their wisdom, the trickster with their pranks and the lover through communion. The king expresses the characteristics of these archetypes and he himself also lives in a transcendental condition. He considers himself merely a vehicle through which all sentient beings can have benefits. By means of his presence, he renders this great energy accessible to all. This mentality is clearly present in the figures of Buddha, Jesus, Mohammed and also in more earthly characters, for example, Martin Luther King and Gandhi.

The second function of the king/queen is to see and bless people, recognizing and valuing everyone for what they are. They, therefore, promote their self-actualization and their fertility, mediating vital forces so that people can truly become what they are. It was typical in Egypt that the king saw his people, in particular moments, as still happens today in Saint Peter's Square in Rome when the Pope sees the crowd, offering his blessing and people feel themselves seen, in a certain sense appreciated, not because they saw the Pope but because they feel seen by him. Feeling valued is an important step towards self-actualization. And when the king sees a person, he is seeing a present and future king in that person.

The figure of the king/queen is wrapped in such powerful energy that approaching them should be done with extreme caution. We know something about this from the legend of the hunter Actaeon who, just by looking at the divinity Diana, who was naked while taking a bath, was turned into a stag and chased by his own dogs. We also learn, according to the legend, that Semele was struck by the look of Zeus when she dared to question who was his favourite consort. For this reason, the energy of the king or queen must be contained, for example, confining it by a red carpet, a protected regal room, not accessible to all, and even on a more daily level, by the wedding ring, which means that this person is, in a certain sense, 'off limits', in other words, already taken.

The shadow side of the king is the tyrant, he who does not convey rules and blessings but makes these energies his own, fooling himself that he was born with them and that whoever receives them will become his faithful servant. This type of king or queen is afflicted with an overdose of narcissism and continues to think, as happens in childhood, that they are the centre of the world. It is the figure of the boy, the eternal child in the film *The Emerald Forest*, who, only after a ritual of initiation, becomes an adult by allowing his infantile part to die.

The tyrant is usually an armour that hides an extremely weak part. It is the scene in *Star Wars* movie in which Darth Vader, Luke Skywalker's father, asks Luke to help him remove his mask, only to reveal an absolutely helpless and impotent face.

EMPATHY AND COMPASSION

30

We can choose whether to meet adversity with fear and hatred or with empathy and compassion.

Empathy refers to the ability of a sentient being to feel the other, that is, to feel the other's emotional state both of pleasure and, in particular, of pain. A common example is when we see someone suffer for whatever cause and we too begin to suffer. Or while we look at a person in an extreme condition, for example, a trapeze artist who is performing a dangerous movement, and we are also tense as if we were on the rope with them. From a neuroscientific point of view, what happens is that the mere fact of seeing what they are doing activates in us the same neurons that are firing in them.

We seem to have a tendency to identify with others at a deep level. This ancient mechanism begins early in life and, perhaps, characterizes all mammals. Taking a tour of a neonatal ward in a hospital, it is common to hear that when one baby starts crying, everyone else participates in this chorus. Empathy is thought to involve certain areas of the limbic brain, the part that has existed for more than a 100 million years. It is a mechanism that could have been born as a way of defending ourselves in the presence of dangers, and today, it has become a feature that is innate in humans.

This natural process is a kind of fusion of one person with another, not at a rational level but more at an organic and energetic level, below the tip of the iceberg, that is, at the unconscious level. It gives us more direct access to the unknown parts of the other, in particular to the emotional states that they are experiencing. It allows us to be in their shoes, that is, not just to think we know what they are experiencing, but to experience reality through their senses. The techniques of neuroimaging show that when we identify with other people, our brains are activated in a way similar to theirs.

A well-known experiment was conducted by taking two portions of yogurt from the same jar and connecting them to a device, the so-called polygraph, an instrument that could measure small changes in the flow of current. When one of the portions was fed with milk, which is food for the bacteria that lives in yogurt, the other portion also showed a galvanic response.

Empathy is, therefore, something that is innate. As far back as prehistoric times, the hunter would activate an empathic connection with the prey by putting themselves, ceremonially, in the animal's shoes. They would wear, for example, its skins and perform ritualistic dances to get more in touch with the animal. Some forms of hunting that date back to the time of the hominids, that is, before homo sapiens, took this union to an even more intimate level. In the procedure called stalking, the hunter followed the footsteps of the prey to enter into a deeper connection, even with its soul. All this was done with great respect, so much so that ceremonies were also held as a sign of respect and gratitude for the animal which, 'graciously', had given itself as food to ensure that the tribe could continue to survive.

In today's world, sometimes, characterized by too much rationality, cultivating empathy is neglected. People are reduced to talking heads, and even when there are animated discussions going on, there is still a remarkable distance between the participants.

But if we really want to fully understand our interlocutor, we need to be consciously in their shoes. This also contributes to a good interpersonal relationship, useful both in personal and professional life. And fortunately, this ability can be trained.

Native Americans talk about walking a mile in the other's moccasins. Literally speaking, we can know, on an intuitive level, how that person places their feet on the ground, and more metaphorically, how they touch the universe, in other words, what connection they have with the surrounding environment.

Another form of training is to observe a picture and imagine the emotional state of the artist while they were painting it. This is what the philosopher Theodor Lipps called *einfühlung*, a German word, whose diffusion was largely responsible for the revival of the concept of empathy in the early years of the 20th century.

Empathy, as we have seen, is not so much an intellectual process but more of a connection at the level of the body and, therefore, at the level of energy. And since it resides in all of us, when activated spontaneously, it could take us by surprise. In these circumstances, it is like being without a rudder and we feel sucked into the other's energy field, we suffer as much as they do, sometimes, more than them, maybe magnifying their discomfort in our imagination. Some professions that have to do with caring for others, for example, nurses or psychologists, are particularly susceptible to this condition and, according to the statistics, at least 60 per cent of this category undergoes the phenomenon of 'burnout' that manifests itself as stress and emotional exhaustion.

These are the moments when compassion is needed. Compassion, according to its etymology, means sharing the passion of another sentient being. Passion refers, again, according to its etymology, to the ability to bear suffering. So, compassion is not feeling the other but feeling with or for the other, especially in their moments of suffering. Compassion is needed to be able to dedicate ourselves to others, enhancing their dreams and aspirations, understanding what they need and, potentially, offering ourselves to them. While empathy is more affective and, often, happens without our realizing it, compassion is more cognitive, rational as it is the process of identification with the needs of others. The underlying reasoning is that nobody should be condemned to suffer unnecessarily or excessively, so we wish them well and, if possible, we work with more awareness to alleviate their condition of suffering.

In this way, we can be compassionate even with those we don't know and even with those who are unpleasant and hostile. It is also a nice way to radiate positivity in the world. We realize that we are all in the same boat, a boat which is inevitably sinking, sooner for some, later for others and, so, we start cheering for each other. We realize, especially in these moments, that life is not eternal and this awareness can, sometimes, be enough to facilitate a deeper and more authentic connection between sentient beings.

One way to increase compassion is to visualize someone we love and to imagine that we are wishing well-being and happiness to that person. Then we continue visualizing someone who is more distant from us and we extend the same wish. Then we view an entire population, even of strangers, and extend compassion even to them. Finally, we address the same wish to ourselves. Compassion towards ourselves is to be considered fundamental and, according to some studies, even more important than self-esteem. It allows us to accept ourselves as we are and to forgive ourselves for our shortcomings. This is a solid starting point for any attempt to improve.

Unlike pity, which makes us feel superior to those in difficulty, often because we are afraid to end up like them, compassion allows us an attitude of forgiveness with respect to others. We realize that everyone has their own story and, sometimes, the only way that the person finds to express themselves is by hurting others. Hurt people, it is said, hurt other people. We can sincerely wish the person to find a more ecological way to bring themselves greater well-being in the future.

This is an altruistic way of living, a source of enormous satisfaction, and it is also demonstrated scientifically that altruism and generosity are responsible for authentic and lasting happiness in humans. It even allows us to raise the level of dopamine and serotonin in our body making us feel more motivated. It would be something to keep alive in children, who already have it but forget it or lose it while growing up, risking, for example, to become bullies to defend their territory against those who are not part of their group.

Offering compassion is not to try to solve the problem that the other is going through. Maybe, someone has a broken heart, but that does not mean that the person is sick or is, in some way, broken. We can simply offer ourselves by expressing our solidarity, our listening and even our understanding without trying to offer solutions or advice or trying to diminish the entity of their problematic condition. We can reassure them that there is nothing wrong in feeling that way and remind them that this too will pass.

GRAMMAR OF COMPASSION

I need
You need
Everyone* needs

to
love
be respected
have joy and fun
be loved and honoured
be taken into consideration
be economically comfortable
be in good mental and physical shape
have intimate and rewarding relationships
have a purpose, a goal for living/working
be stimulated and therefore learn new things
be part of a vital community of friends/colleagues
be in contact with life's forces and with his own divinity

---

* *Adults, children, men, women, black, white, red, yellow, rich, poor, Buddhist, Jews.*

MIRROR NEURONS

When neurons fire together, they wire together.

—*Donald Hebb*

Mirror neurons were discovered thanks to the work of Giacomo Rizzolatti and his team around the year 1990 at the University of Parma, Italy. In their experiments with macaque monkeys, whose neocortex is similar to that of the human being, they noticed a strange phenomenon. It was already well-known that when we perform an action, for example, when we grab an object, certain specific neurons are activated in our brain. One day, a colleague of Rizzolatti was walking around the lab and picked up something in his hand. At the same time, in one of the monkeys that was quietly waiting for her new task, an activity took place in her brain, as if she were herself taking hold of an object, even though there was nothing in sight to grasp. The monkey was putting herself in the shoes of the person she was watching.

If being in the shoes of another person is a consequence of mirror neurons, then it would be enough, when we are with other people, to activate them and thereby put ourselves in their shoes, so as to facilitate a more authentic and profound empathic relationship. It is, therefore, necessary to let our body be guided by the other. To facilitate this process, we can simulate their gestures in our body, that is, mapping their body onto ours. The result is that we will experience what the other is experiencing. At a level below the conscious, that is, without any rational processing, we will be able to inhabit their world, be behind their eyes, in their skin so we can finally be able to understand another human being. We will be able to understand not only their words, but their intentions, state of mind and the energy that conveys their words, but only after having experienced these states within us.

This is not a rational process and goes far beyond being able to read the mind of another, a concept which should be understood only figuratively, not to be taken literally. Trying to read the mind of another person is too complex a task for a normal human being, given the immense quantity of data that each person processes at any time. The small changes, for example, that occur in a person's posture and gestures are all important but often go unnoticed when we try to make sense of what they are saying.

Mapping their body, that is, reproducing their gestures and posture to activate the same neurons in us as the ones they are using, is an operation that occurs through mirroring. This entails matching their movements. At first, it might seem artificial because we have to consciously follow their gestures, but over time, it becomes quite natural, as it is for children who naturally like imitation games. This also applies to adults who, by lending themselves to this game, immediately become more likeable in the eyes of children.

While mirroring for children may seem like imitation, even if many other mechanisms that concern awareness are involved, for adults it should be done with the intention and the great curiosity of knowing the other person more intimately, honouring them, valuing them and giving all our attention to what they are communicating. To mirror respectfully, it is advisable to wait about three seconds before starting the movement, as happens in life when we are not aware that we are mirroring.

By doing it too soon, it could be interpreted as an intention to manipulate.

The activation of mirror neurons communicates to the other person that we are like them, and mirroring means we want to be even more like them. A curious application of this technique is found in the case of the amputation of a limb. When the person feels itching in the limb that is not there, if we scratch our limb at the point where the other says they feel the itch, it is as if they too scratch themselves and they usually find relief. Of course, mirroring is not just for therapeutic uses but serves to shorten the distance between two people and, in general, to put ourselves in the other person's shoes. It is a sort of bio-indicator of the degree of empathy and intimacy. The more people like each other, the more they reflect each other's moves.

Even when reading a novel, the reader may feel involved in simulating actions described in the text. This act of identifying oneself, typical of mirror neurons, is what actors also do to enter a character, even to hear, as Tom Hanks claims to have done in the movie *Castaway*, the voice of the ball, Wilson, talking to him.

The parts of the body that lend themselves most immediately to being mirrored are the head with its inclination, shoulders, legs and feet with their positioning and the distribution of our body weight. The facial expression as well, that is, how the persons wiggle their nose, how they purse their lips and how they frown are all actions that can be mirrored. All these aspects are related to the reasoning process that is going on inside the person, without their necessarily realizing it.

Another aspect of empathy that can be seen when two people are in tune is that their rates of breathing align. This phenomenon, also known in some circles as the breath of the choir, is reminiscent of the symbiotic relationship between mother and newborn especially during breastfeeding. It could be used to facilitate empathic relationships even among adults. It is necessary to observe, with relaxed eyes and without staring invasively, the rhythm of the interlocutor's breath by noticing how their chest moves and simply starting to breathe at the same rate. A feeling of commonality is guaranteed, and this often allows the mirroring of other parts of the body to work with naturalness.

A more advanced and more evolved technique is an indirect one called cross-over mirroring. When it is not easy to mirror explicitly, maybe, because a person feels too observed, it can be done using another part of the body. If the person nods or moves their eyelids, these attitudes can be mirrored with a similar movement of the hand. Milton Erickson, the doctor who was most responsible for re-launching hypnosis as a therapeutic approach, was an expert in the elegant use of mirroring. One day, a patient of his did not want to sit but continued to walk nervously back and forth. Erickson mirrored this, taking a pencil between two of his fingers and moving it so that it looked natural, but doing so at the same pace as his patient's walk. When the empathic connection was formed, that is, the mirror neurons were activated and both had become, as Bateson would have said, parts of the same plot, Erickson began to slow down the movement of his pencil and the patient slowed down his frantic pace. At one point, Erickson completely stopped the movement while the patient was in front of a chair and, at that moment, it was easy to invite him to sit down.

In addition, the voice with its tonality, tempo, timbre, volume and melody has its importance in the mirroring and activation of mirror neurons. The qualities that are more immediately reproducible are speed and volume. As can easily be understood, if a person speaks rather quickly and their interlocutor very slowly, almost in slow motion, it is very likely that who speaks fast will grow impatient, failing to convey the sense of what they want to say, while the slower one will fail to receive the message being conveyed. The same is true for the volume, if one is screaming, perhaps in anger, and the other speaks almost quietly, with the positive intention of calming down the situation, it is more than likely that the one who is screaming will scream even more because they will not feel understood. An example in the family is a parent's habit of wanting to wake up their son by shouting good morning while the young one's eyes are still full of sleep. The parent risks creating a shock, like receiving a slap as soon as one opens their eyes. A more useful technique, for example when two people are speaking at different paces, is to reflect the mood and vocal qualities of the other and gradually accelerate them. The other party usually follows suit so as to recreate or maintain the synchrony between those involved.

It is not possible to say exactly why mirror neurons are activated, but it can certainly be hypothesized what happens. The most accredited thesis indicates that a relationship develops between the people in which both feel no longer as two separate 'I's but connected, as if part of the weave of a shared complex design. It is the condition of interdependence that translates into a form of structural coupling, a phenomenon that occurs between living elements that are together. This creates changes in each of the parts, as can be heard in the song of birds in the forest or in a group that is playing jazz.

And this is the basis of the empathic relationship which, according to the well-known neuroscientist V. S. Ramachandran, is essential for the survival of sociable beings such as primates and humans.

33   ATTACHMENT

Take off proudly into the light, without looking back.

We live in a condition that the Buddhist nun Pema Chodron defines as the fundamental ambiguity of being human. We want novelty and, at the same time, we don't want things to change. Maybe, we do not mind changing an old suit, a pair of shoes or a car. But for some people, even learning a foreign language could already be too big a challenge, perhaps we have to put certain skills into play in order to produce sounds that are not natural but which perhaps, could, at times, bring our thinking closer to that of the people whose sounds we are aiming to reproduce. Not to mention unlearning, that is, leaving certain old habits behind and re-learning, in other words, adding new ways of behaving.

In general, to modify some aspect of our being, if there is not a good prize in sight, we encounter several difficulties. We are attached to our sense of self and we need to keep it stable throughout our life, ensuring that its shape and configuration remain as familiar as possible. We retrace known mental paths and, sometimes, fiercely justify that these are the only correct ones. We force the interpretation of reality according to our point of view and we become dogmatic, unable to tolerate uncertainty. This attachment to the status quo, on the one hand, gives us comfort, but on the other, it makes us much more fragile in a world that is constantly changing. It is a fragility that, if not adequately addressed, leads us to react by withdrawing from reality or to attack it with extreme force and vehemence, constantly trying to bring reality back to a dimension that is more comfortable for us.

We are afraid, for example, that if we lose in a debate, it means that we will be dominated by the adversary, whom we immediately paint as an enemy, ready to annihilate us. So, we insist on bringing even extraneous elements in our discourse, we throw, as was used in the fox hunt, some red herrings on the course to divert the competitors' dogs onto false tracks. The stronger the emotional impact, the more we deviate from the thread of the discourse, and the only thing that matters, at this point, is to demonstrate, at all costs, that the interlocutor is wrong, sticking to the belief that we are right. Maybe, we get angry, raise the tone of our voice, our heart rate increases and we may even appear red in the face. And the more we insist, the more we find ourselves in a vortex of emotions from which it becomes increasingly difficult to exit. Every move, at this point, becomes like trying to put out a fire by pouring kerosene on it.

Sometimes, these reactions happen in situations that other people might think are really inexplicable. Our companion, for example, may squeeze the toothpaste tube in a way that we do not approve, our friend may jingle the coins or the keys in their pocket making a noise that we find unpleasant, a word may be spoken with a particular tone of voice or accompanied by a particular gesture. These are all situations that, perhaps, once might well have been a source of attraction to us but, now, they have become unfriendly and hostile, powerful enough to cause an eruption.

In these cases, it is again the attachment to the sense of our identity that is seriously under threat. We divide the world rigidly into two categories, the I, the one who is right, and the non-I, or the others, those who are wrong. Even after knowing that insisting on trying to prove that we are right we are only putting up more barriers in a dialogue, we find a strange pleasure in insisting on doing so. We defend our political or idealistic movement, even denigrating the opponent and this makes us feel even righter and more righteous, but no one is listening to us. It is like scratching the bite of a mosquito in the hope of instant relief, knowing that we are only aggravating the itch. Or it is the alcoholic who knows they should not drink but despite this, is attracted to the bottle, and as the poet Shantideva said, they do not want suffering but, unfortunately, love what is causing it.

A curious thing, perhaps we can say due to the poverty of language, is when we talk about my wife, my husband, my son. The use of the possessive adjective seems to give us the right to possess the thing to which the adjective refers. We even talk about my car, and when we take a plane, of my flight, which, if it was late, causes us not little suffering. We feel attacked, some may even feel annihilated, they feel the world takes no account of them. Would it be better to say, for example, the flight I would like to take, the car I drive, the son to me?

This inability to get out of this state of being hijacked, the extreme attachment to just one modality of operation is called *shenpa* in Sanskrit language. It can be traced to a limited and exclusive map of the self, a rigid judgment, often at the level of the unconscious, that separates us from others and describes us as desirable or undesirable, deserving or undeserving. It is a rigid division that we hope to preserve to maintain order in our lives. For some, it could represent the hope of arriving first in the alleged race towards happiness through consensus and the approval of others.

Attachment also manifests itself in forms that appear benign. For example, there is the bookworm who does not enjoy life in the open air because they have to dig even more deeply into the matter that they are studying. Or there are those who have to convert every single sentence into a work of inner reflection, perpetually questioning themselves. Another example is the eternal student who, as soon as they finish a course of study, sets out in a desperate search of a new one, not so much because they are convinced that they do not know enough, but because they would not know what to do if they should abandon the attachment to studies. There is of course also the attachment to work, money, power and sex.

But this life, as Schopenhauer said referring to the numerous upheavals that we have to go through, is something that shouldn't had been. It is a business that does not even cover its costs. We often find ourselves in the dark wood of Dante, having lost the right way and this happens not only in the middle of the journey of our life. Things that were not contemplated and not foreseen are thrown onto our path, inviting us to stop, observe, learn and grow. They are things which serve to thicken the soup of life, making it, paradoxically, more agreeable. And so, the invitation comes again, even without going to look for it, to undertake another journey of continuous improvement.

The awareness that it is time to leave an attachment could arise because we begin to feel certain sensations that are typical of being kidnapped. Some symptoms are excessive tension in the body, a lump in the throat or in the solar plexus, increased body temperature, the sensation of not feeling the ground under our feet, or like being in quicksand, or for some, like walking on fish. A constant is that the status quo is seriously threatened. We feel we must find something solid where we can regain stability, maintaining the sense of a well intact ego, and, in a sense, even superior to the others.

But if we realize the interconnection that exists between all sentient beings, we succeed in going beyond the illusion of separation between the I and the non-I. We realize that there are over seven billion ways of living this human existence, and we also realize that there is not only one right way, but it is a question of identifying which are the most useful ways, the most appropriate ones to promote a condition of greater well-being for all. Taking a few breaths to rebalance our system, we also begin to realize our fragility, to realize that we are in the same boat with everyone else and we feel like cheering them on as well. Everyone is trying in their own way, sometimes short-sightedly, to improve their condition, to suffer less. We become more human and less arrogant. We will no longer be alone, each attached to their own ego. We will be able to lose ourselves in a more useful way in the dance of life without the dancer having, at all costs, to show off, because when the dance is beautiful, the world is more interested in the dance than in the dancer.

With this, we will not be able to eliminate problems, but their power and their stronghold over us will decrease in a remarkable way. And we will be able to intervene better and with more objectivity on injustices, managing our fury and minimizing any obstinacy and attachment.

Letting go of attachment, especially towards ourselves, apart from making our lives sweeter and more compassionate, is also an excellent preparation for the final act, when in the words of the poet Tagore, we will be ready to return the keys of the house that we have inhabited for a lifetime and give up all our claims.

And so, the wave that seemed so big and threatening gets smaller and smaller, finally disappearing.

34   CURIOSITY

Somewhere, something extraordinary is waiting to be discovered.

—Carl Sagan

Life, said the philosopher Kierkegaard, is not a problem to be solved but a mystery to be experienced and appreciated. It is a mystery for which, as the word itself says, we have no definite answers, if not temporarily. We often find ourselves having to settle for a conclusion, a thesis while waiting for new explorations, new results, which can confirm our thesis, modify it or even turn it completely on its head. Uncertainty accompanies us, given that the only constant is change, and while this may be inconvenient, on the other hand, it is an essential part of what keeps us alive. We live a life that becomes more interesting, precisely, because we do not know exactly what the next moment will bring.

A quality that can be useful on this journey is curiosity. One of its definitions is the restless or inconvenient desire to seek and know the affairs of others and what does not belong to us, whether for the love of truth or of gossip. Focusing on the first aspect, the love of truth, we immediately realize that the search will be endless. According to the physicist Niels Bohr, the opposite of a truth could be another equally important truth. What we commonly call truth is, often, the result of having unconsciously filtered aspects of the millions of bits of information that arrive to us from the world. In so doing, we come to conclusions that could be different from those of other people who filter differently. They could also be different from the very conclusions that we will reach when our filters change, a process that happens when a person begins to question themselves.

Curiosity, not so much as a skill or a competence but more as a way of being in life, allows us to understand better our surroundings and to find new solutions to problems. But, above all, it allows us to get to know people better. They too are part of the great mystery. Indeed, it is enough to look into the eyes of a child, who is just a few months of age, to appreciate the vast infinity that resides inside them. And maybe, we can, according to William Blake, 'See a world in a grain of sand and paradise in a wild flower, hold the infinite in the palm of our hand and eternity in an hour.' This way of living everyday life is not automatic for most people when faced with something new, because it requires us to be still for a little longer than we usually are. Perhaps, even going beyond our comfort zone to enter the area of curiosity, that area in which answers are not immediate and where we may return, even if only momentarily, to the state of the innocent child, devoid of filters and preconceptions.

One way to train this curiosity is through the following questions, which do not give rise to definite answers, but allow for the meeting of different points of view. We may ask ourselves, from time to time, for example, what will happen next month or how will the human being be 50 years from now. Other questions that can lead us to reflect and examine our beliefs, avoiding reaching conclusions that are too hasty, can be what is the mind, what is love, how did we arrive in this human life and why are we still here. The writer Mark Twain used to say, in his typically humorous tone, that there are only two important dates to remember, the first is day we were born, the second is the day when we discover why we were born.

An important consideration if we wanted to utilize these questions with another person is to appreciate their answers before offering our own. Conversations, too often, even among developed adults, can be likened to the habit typical of the world of animals, dogs in particular, that is, to mark one's own territory. A person declaring something as their own truth may immediately assume the air of infallibility and incontestability. Almost as a reflex action, another person feels as though called to say their own piece, over-marking the recently marked territory. And so, it goes on without reaching any conclusion, except to prove who has the strongest voice and thereby manages to dominate. Waiting before answering with the curiosity to see the meaning in what the other is saying is the basis of a good dialogue, in other words, creating a meaning that derives from the sum of the different points of view.

Albert Einstein said he had no particular talents but that he was passionately curious. Developing this way of being can also be facilitated by immersing ourselves in nature, for example, being in front of an extreme phenomenon like a waterfall, sunset, or after having walked for hours to reach the top of a mountain and appreciating the immensity of the firmament above and the view of the countryside below. Even the night offers a fascinating experience, when we find ourselves where there is no artificial lighting and we are looking at the stars. Most people feel a sense of wonder, accompanied maybe by a sigh, a breath that goes much deeper than usual and, for a moment, we lose our sense of self because we find ourselves in a context infinitely greater than the confines of our daily life. There is also a momentary loss of the sense of time, we do not realize that time is passing, and we find ourselves in a state of immense grace in which all judgment is suspended and there is no need to reach a conclusion.

A benefit of this kind of experience is to be able to face life with greater interest and openness. It allows us to live better through ambiguity and uncertainty. We become less dogmatic and we are better able to appreciate diversity, a basic requirement for peaceful coexistence among the over seven billion human beings on this planet.

So, when we meet another person, we can look at them with fresh, open eyes. According to the tradition of the troubadours of the 12th century, the eyes are the explorers of the heart. The heart sends the eyes to scout for a pleasant image. When they find one, they offer it to the heart and if the heart is kind, love is born. For some, curiosity, whose root is in the word 'cure', is also a matter of the heart. This is a connection that can bring two people, if not to love each other and lose themselves in the other, certainly to a level of mutual trust, which is the basis of any good interpersonal relationship.

But curiosity, even though it could involve the heart, does not mean digging into the other person, harassing and dissecting them with questions. Such an attitude could represent the ruthless, perhaps, inhuman aspect of scientific research, comparable to the scalpel of a surgeon invading the patient's body, an intervention that is not easily tolerable without anaesthesia.

It is, therefore, necessary to manage our curiosity, first with silence, almost in a meditative state. Silence is a prerequisite for listening and discovering things we didn't know and the things we didn't know that we didn't know, without jumping to conclusions. Some reflections that facilitate this state, for example, when we meet someone, could be contemplating who they really are, what are their dreams and what is their gift, the uniqueness that they can offer to the world. These are questions to which we don't have immediate answers and require a certain presence and a certain curiosity to keep them alive.

Finally, we would like to be able to say, with the famous writer Mary Oliver, that all our life we were like a bride married to amazement.

WHERE ATTENTION GOES

Who has a hammer sees everything as a nail.

Perhaps, we remember that while we were thinking about buying a certain model of a car, we began to see many examples of that model in circulation. It is not that they were not around before, it is just that we simply didn't pay attention to them. The same applies when choosing a holiday, we begin to notice posters in different parts of the city that advertise the very journey that we were thinking of.

Another example of this phenomenon, known to do-it-yourself enthusiasts, is by roaming around their home with a hammer or screwdriver in hand, they begin to notice how many nails or screws need to be attended to. Indeed, by paying specific attention, a word whose Latin etymology means to stretch towards a certain direction, certain aspects tend to be more noticed, to be singled out, thus, excluding those that are not included in the scope of our attention. Not surprisingly, it is said that whoever has a hammer sees everything as nails. Or that if a pickpocket meets a saint, they don't see anything other than their pockets.

Our attention also directs us when driving a vehicle. When we go around a curve on a motorcycle, for example, the vehicle goes according to where we are looking. If the motorcyclist is distracted by other vehicles circulating in the opposite direction, their own vehicle will tend to deviate from its path and be attracted towards the other vehicles. This phenomenon can also be seen when driving in fog where visibility is next to nothing.

If we encounter a vehicle that is coming from the opposite direction, the tendency may be to look at its headlights, that being the only certainty we have in such conditions. The risk is, of course, to collide with the other car.

The postulate behind this is that our energy flows where attention goes. To put it another way, what we appreciate gets appreciated. As in nature, if we continue to care for a plant, it is more likely to grow and flourish than another plant that does not receive any nourishment and which will, consequently, wither away.

An example of what it means to devote attention is when we have to solve a problem. If we continue to think about the problem and its negative consequences, maybe accompanied by a hint of pessimism, the problem will seem to grow. It is likely that we will come to think that there is no solution and we risk finding ourselves in a state of negativity and impotence. If instead, once the structure of the problem has been analysed, breaking it down into its symptoms and causes, we shift our attention to the solution we want to achieve, we manage to find easier ways to get out of the prison in which the problem is detaining us and the possibility of finding a solution increases. If our attention is intensely directed towards a solution, even visualizing ourselves already with the solution in hand, the prefrontal cortex in the brain becomes activated. This is the part of the brain that does not know the difference between past, present and future and acts as if the problem has already been solved, thereby giving us the confidence that goes with a successful experience, even if it has not yet happened. In this way, we are less weighed down by the gravity of the problem and, consequently, we will be freer to make choices in a more rational way.

This is not an encouragement to neglect the extent of a problem, as happens in some work contexts. With the good intention of not wanting to contaminate the environment and people with even more emotional overload, some people avoid pronouncing the word problem, speaking instead of opportunities. This is a misleading reasoning because problems that are not mentioned could remain like skeletons in the closet, ready to leap out at us when we least expect them. It is also an insidious reasoning because it may be disrespectful to someone who is suffering or simply asking for some support. We risk giving the impression that we are playing down the extent of the problem and to a certain extent, not giving sufficient attention to the person who has the problem. Not surprisingly, it is said that problems will not go away until they have taught us everything there is to learn from them.

A more useful way to talk about problems is to talk about them in terms of the problematic condition, that is, how we are traversing the problematic state. In this way, we render a problem more dynamic, something that could worsen or lessen. In addition, we may say that the person has a problem, not that the person is a problem, and this is a fine distinction that keeps the person's self-esteem intact. Even a pessimist might begin to be more convinced that there is a way out and others who, superficially, think that it is better to ignore the problem in the hope that it goes away will be tempted to devote more attention to facilitate the problem to move on. What would be appropriate in these circumstances is to allow those who are in the problematic state, maybe even suffering, to traverse the moment with more resources. It should, therefore, be remembered that the situation is calling the person to pay more attention to certain aspects of themselves and their life that they had neglected up until this point in time.

The same reasoning applies to diseases. Western medicine, by tradition, gives a lot of attention to symptoms and little to the state of well-being. It is assumed that once the prescribed drug is taken, the patient will be fine, and it is unlikely that the doctor will conduct a follow up on the patient's health once the drug has been taken. This bias in favour of illness is due, in part, to university studies where the first contact with the human body is not with a living and healthy one but with corpses on which to experiment. The metaphor of medicine is fighting disease rather than promoting health. Although it could be argued that the intention is the same, the focus on the disease could have the effect of keeping the person still trapped in the agony of suffering. Any attempt to combat an illness risks highlighting it, increasing our worries and concerns. The opposite of illness, that is health, recedes into the background, almost unnoticed, precisely, because our energy flows where our attention goes.

From the point of view of neuroscience, when attention is given to a stimulus, the neural response to that stimulus increases. Consequently, other neurons, those not involved in the object of attention, are quieted. The reticular activating system (RAS) gets stimulated and alerts the brain about what we consider important and what we want. This system is on the lookout for evidence that confirms our focus. An example is when we read a page of a book, where there are black characters and blank or white spaces. Our RAS informs us how to distribute our attention between these two aspects. We pay more attention to the letters, that is, the lines and the curves in black, and ignore the white spaces between the letters. When we give our attention to the letters, that is, we take care of them, the signals in the brain that correspond to this activity are strengthened, compared to what we are not paying attention to, namely, the white spaces. These do not get represented in our brain and the neuronal activity associated with them is drastically reduced, perhaps, even leaving no trace in our memory. We do not, in actual fact, remember the white spaces between the letters and the words.

Paying attention, in one way or another, creates changes in the structure and functioning of the nervous system. It means that we choose how our mind will work, we choose, in a very real sense, who we want to be in the next moment. It could be said that at any time, according to where and how we direct our attention, we are creating our future.

In this connection, there is the story of a grandfather who tells his grandson that he feels like he was torn between two wolves who were living inside him. One is good and does no harm. It lives in harmony with all that surrounds it and does not waste its energy on injustices but acts in appropriate ways. The other wolf, on the other hand, is full of sorrows. The most insignificant situation succeeds in generating a state of anger in him. He is always belligerent and this, often, dulls his mind. But he is impotent in his anger and is unable to change anything. For the grandfather, it is a continuous challenge to manage these two wolves because they both try to dominate his spirit.

When the grandson asks him which one wins, he replies that it simply depends on which one he chooses to feed and nurture.

Fortunately, attention is not a fixed thing, we can pay attention in one direction and then recall it to give it in another direction. After examining what is preventing us from achieving our goals, we can decide which is the most useful direction to nurture.

To conclude, here is a story from the Zen tradition. A student asks the master to write one gem of great wisdom. The master writes the word, 'Attention'. The student asks if there is not something else to add, to which the master writes, 'Attention, Attention'. When the student concludes that this does not seem to be of great wisdom, the master writes, 'Attention, Attention, Attention'.

36 TYPES OF ATTENTION

Energy flows according to where and how we pay attention. It can flow towards something, something external, or it can be directed internally, within us. It can be directed towards a single point, a single zone, in other words, in a confined and narrow way, or it can be broadened and expanded to include more aspects of a situation. Each of these modes leads to different ways of processing reality, each of which creates mental maps that can be, more or less, appropriate and with which we can intervene to manage life's situations in more useful ways.

Directing our attention also involves changing the boundaries of the self. When it is directed externally, for example, it can include more aspects of the outside world, while directing it internally, it can exclude these aspects in favour of others, as if we were listening only to ourselves. Our attention tends to be very selective, and based on this, we give meaning to the universe. Its selectivity depends, in addition to the direction, on the filters we apply which include language, culture and our personal experience. The result is that we see, hear, feel, taste and smell certain things, certain aspects of life, and ignore all that is not in our sphere of attention, we ignore what does not concern us, we could say. If we are looking for things like, for example, a certain colour, we tend not to see the other colours around us. Everything we do not see, says Judith DeLozier, co-founder of neurolinguistic programming, looks the same.

With a greater awareness of how we use our attention, we will know how to direct it more appropriately according to the situation in which we find ourselves. We will be able to direct it outwards, inwards, in a narrow or in a broad or wide manner. According to the latest research in neuroscience, all this means more flexibility, the main portal towards neuroplasticity, a word that eloquently describes our ability to update and change.

When we do not direct our attention appropriately, we risk being at the mercy of distractions. In such cases, there is an increase in our energy consumption. The time to complete a job, for example, is extended by 25 per cent and there is also a price to pay, in terms of glucose consumption, when we shift our attention from one thing to another. We hardly succeed in giving attention to two activities simultaneously, the so-called phenomenon of multitasking. We instead do, what is called, sequential tasking, that is, we switch between the two activities in rapid succession.

And it seems that the duration of our attention has decreased from 12 seconds in 2000 to 8 seconds in 2013. That of a goldfish is still 9 seconds.

Four types of attention are described below. We have the ability to switch between one and another, but what is needed is the awareness regarding the kind of attention we are using.

EXTERNAL ATTENTION

External attention, as the word itself says, means directing our energy outside us. It could be directed towards a part of the environment around us, for example, towards a person with whom we wish to enter into a more authentic or profound relationship. In this case, we will begin to pay more attention to how they express themselves, their gestures, tone of voice and the language they use to express their thoughts. We will have to put more emphasis on our interlocutor, expanding the sphere of our awareness, no longer centred on us but to include the other. In some moments, we will dedicate a bit more energy to ourselves, for example, when we want not only to listen but to articulate a concept. In this sense, a dialogue becomes a sort of dance in which both people move in concert. At times, we will feel one with the other, at other times, separate and so on. The way in which we place our attention creates a continuous modification of boundaries of the self.

Professional sportspeople who use mechanical means, bicycles, motorcycles and cars, though not being aware of this game of attention, use it to become one with their vehicles. Paying attention externally allows the body to self-organize and to regulate movement better and more automatically, without having to think about the movements themselves. When a racing car driver travels along a curve, a significant part of the self is to be found in the rim of the steering wheel, in the point of contact where the rubber meets the road and even in the contact between their bottom and the car seat. These points of contact become extensions of the self, a self whose boundaries are constantly changing, sometimes, even retracting according to the needs of the moment.

A correct use of external attention also serves to reach a destination or to achieve a goal. Traveling along a street, we focus on signs, other vehicles and any obstacles that are to be avoided or overcome. If it happens, as it does sometimes, that we do not see an exit on the highway, although clearly marked, we will say that we were distracted or absent minded. It means that we were present elsewhere, really, our attention might have been directed towards a conversation we were having while driving. The direction of attention is also to be taken into account when pursuing more conceptual objectives, for example, managing a project. The outcome should be constantly kept in focus, perhaps, by looking at it with more attention to its details and continuing to monitor its progress, minimizing the inevitable distractions that are always lurking.

INTERNAL ATTENTION

Internal attention means dealing with what happens inside our body. This allows us to have greater awareness of how we manage ourselves, for example, in the areas of health and well-being. According to the assumption that the relationship between the body and mind is such that each of these aspects influences the other, paying attention internally allows us to focus more on some of those parts which are responsible for or, in some way, related to our state of health. This takes some training but it becomes easier after taking a few breaths, maybe counting how many breaths we managed to take in a minute.

In this state where there will be more internal attention, we can activate biofeedback. We can imagine having a conversation with our cells, for example, we can send invitations to speed up or slow down the energy that is circulating inside, to regulate our heart rate, our body temperature and other vital functions. We can also listen to what these parts may be wanting to tell us in their own language, a language that we can decipher if our attention is sufficiently internally directed. Similarly, we can harness the support of our immune system to increase our defences, to expel harmful substances, to facilitate the growth of internal parts and to prevent the growth of other unwanted ones. Exactly as what happens in a healthy body.

All this should be done not with the presumption of dominating our body, but for the sake of facilitating the harmony between the inner and the outer world, a condition that is fundamental for our well-being. Internal attention also allows us to understand if our body is asking us for something to which we are not listening and, therefore, invites us to take the most appropriate remedies.

Internal attention is also important for the awareness of how we perform certain movements that have become habitual over time, especially if we want to change them or improve them. This is about being in contact with even the micro movements that are part of a complete movement and taking action on these. A sportsperson, for example, could direct their attention to fine tune where their gaze is directed or can adjust the perception of their centre of gravity. Minor improvements in micro-areas lead to major improvements in macro-movements.

This is what may be called targeted or smart training, an important practice that avoids doing only mechanical repetitions of a movement in the hope of improvement. It is a technique that is part of the approach of what Tim Gallwey, one of the forerunners of modern coaching, called the inner game. While the outer game, the visible game, concerns the technical skills necessary to perform a job, the inner game concerns the mental processes that allow the technique to be applied. In tennis, for example, according to the inner game approach, the most formidable opponent is not the one on the other side of the net but the one found inside one's own head, the one that is responsible for the movements that the body produces.

In modern times, internal attention has become very lacking. The blame is partially to be placed on the wealth of electronic devices that surround us. Cell phones promise to keep us constantly connected with the rest of the world and social media leads us to immediately express what crossed our mind without as much as a moment's reflection about whether it is a valid and useful move. The consequence is that we live ever more distant from our being and it becomes difficult to remember how to place our attention internally.

Unless we give ourselves permission to take a few deep breaths.

NARROW ATTENTION

Narrow attention serves to focus more sharply and with greater precision and, therefore, to exclude what is superfluous. It may be compared to the zoom function in a camera. Although we can use this type of attention with all our five senses, where it is most readily used is with the visual system. In this case, we are talking about foveal vision, the one that uses the fovea, the central part of the retina. This is an area full of cones that are used to see bright images, their details and colours.

Foveal vision is somewhat similar to tunnel vision and is something we can experience when there is a high degree of absorption in a task, for example, using the computer and not noticing what is happening around, or talking in the car and being so absorbed as to miss the exit on the highway, or even talking to someone and seeing only a few aspects of their face.

This is also the gateway to many meditation practices and it is a way to facilitate internal attention. We can experience it by setting up a timer for a minute and counting the number of in breaths and out breaths we are taking. It is not easy to keep the attention on the numbers, so if we were to lose count, it is sufficient to start over again for another minute. Being able to do this leads us into what is called an altered state in which we are no longer absorbed in the routine of day-to-day life and we are, therefore, less distracted.

A narrow focus is, therefore, on details, on a concentrated area, a point that for an archer would be the target or the bullseye.

The sportsperson, in this condition, manages not to notice the presence of the public, which could be a distraction. The negative aspect of narrow attention is that we may not see an object that is right under our eyes or if we are so focused on achieving a goal, we may ignore the negative effects that this could have on the other people involved.

In summary, a narrow focus and, therefore, foveal vision serves to achieve a goal, reducing or eliminating distractions. This is what we tend to use in moments of intense stress or danger. We filter what is superfluous in order to implement certain inherited mechanisms, namely fight, flight or freeze. Our heart rate increases, there is more adrenaline in the system and the muscles of our arms and legs are ready to act.

After using this mechanism to remove us from danger, we need to regain a state of lucidity, re-oxygenate our brain and be able to capture other useful inputs from the environment that surrounds us. This recovery is even more essential when the danger is not real but a perceived one, like mistaking a stick for a snake, perhaps, because we were in a particularly vulnerable state.

Recovery can be facilitated through the use of broad attention.

BROAD ATTENTION

Broad attention serves instead to include more aspects of a context and, therefore, to be more present and aware of the situations in which we live. This allows us to comprehend more variables and their effect of both short and long term.

As for the visual field, we can talk about peripheral vision which uses rods. This type of vision retrieves the information that was deleted in foveal vision. It is also used to see movements and to see in dim light. It is believed that broad attention and, consequently, peripheral vision involves a part that is out of our conscious sphere and is the part that really manages our well-being. In addition to facilitating better communication between the two hemispheres of the brain, peripheral vision leads to a slowing down of the brain waves, which enters the alpha state, 8–14 Hz. approximately, becoming more regular and synchronized. This generates a state of greater calmness within and, therefore, more readiness to meet the challenges of life.

A good management of our attention, by means of our peripheral vision, frees the mind from anxiety, chronic stress and debilitating concerns. It allows us to learn more fluently because the synaptic junctions between our neurons become stronger.

It is to be noted that peripheral vision, after having developed our narrow and internal attention by means of counting some breaths, also facilitates an altered state, a sort of trance state in which the mind calms down even further and we feel united with more of the entire surrounding context. This was the basic state of many shamanic practices, for example, the Chinese practice 'wu-wei,' and 'stopping the world' of Carlos Castaneda, and it is also a basic condition for martial arts in which giving one's eyes to the opponent means to be immediately captured.

In the altered, relaxed state, with proper training, we will be able to turn off certain areas of brain that could otherwise hinder a successful execution of what we are intent on doing. We could decrease the intensity of pain up to the point of not even feeling it, as happens, for example, when we observe a small cut on our finger without any memory of where and when it may have happened. This state allows us to be so absorbed in what we are doing as to suppress what we think is not important. Broad attention, well managed will, subsequently, allow us to access a good quality of narrow attention, very focused, allowing those parts of us needed to perform a task to work at their very best.

Broad attention, since it includes diverse aspects of a context, is also a good invitation to let our thoughts wander, facilitating distractions that allow us to dream and create. When we daydream, we abandon the executive mode and we regenerate some of the functions of our brain. We can see more clearly connections between things that seemed disconnected. This ability is one of the bases of creativity, that is, being able to generate new connections between events. The synaptic connections between neurons increase and we generate new ones. We are also able to plan a fuller and possibly richer future.

Some valid activities that facilitate daydreaming are listening to music, walking in nature, washing dishes, doing embroidery and even watching something undemanding on television. It also seems that working in a messy room can facilitate this faculty. Einstein's desk is a testament to this.

Finally, speaking of broad attention in women, their peripheral vision extends more easily to 45 degrees on either side. This is an inherited trait that derives from the era of large families. The woman had to take care of everyone, keeping under control what was happening in different corners of the house. Men, on the other hand, prefer foveal vision having inherited it from the days of the hunt when they were focused on the prey, which was necessary for the survival of the family. Even today, men tend to ask where a certain object is in the house, though it may be right under their very eyes, while the woman may find it even blindfolded.

Some modern technologies, for example, television and computers, tend to favour foveal vision to the detriment of the peripheral one.

FEEDBACK

37

> *The illiterate of the future will not be those who cannot read or write, but those who do not know how to learn, unlearn, and learn again.*
>
> —*Alvin Toffler*

Feedback is a mechanism that serves to measure how close a person is approaching a desired result while performing an action. When we are traveling, for example, apart from the road signs and the time elapsed in relation to the forecasted arrival, there are several other indicators that give us feedback on how we are proceeding. Whether we are traveling to the mountains or to the seaside, the scenario, including the vegetation, gradually, begins to resemble that of our destination. In the absence of such feedback, we may deduce that we are on the wrong road.

Scientifically we can talk about two types of feedback, positive and negative. Positive feedback, also called reinforcing feedback, tells us that we are on the right track and to continue doing what we were doing, maybe even better or more. Negative or balancing feedback informs us that we are off course and that our choices and, consequently, our actions are not appropriate so that we can make the necessary changes to get back on track.

Without feedback, it is like driving in fog. Helen Keller, that extraordinary person who, despite being blind and deaf, managed to graduate from Harvard spoke about this fog when she said,

> Have you ever been at sea in a dense fog, when it seemed as if a tangible white darkness shut you in, and the great ship, tense and anxious, groped her way

toward the shore with plummet and sounding-line, and you waited with beating heart for something to happen? I was like that ship before my education began, only I was without compass or sounding-line, and had no way of knowing how near the harbor was.[7]

If the course is well outlined and the objective well formulated, the path taken to get to the desired result could suffice to give us feedback. But when it comes to human interactions, feedback is often offered by a living person, for example, a boss, parent or friend, and that is where problems arise. When a person is involved, our readiness to accept feedback depends largely on the relationship we have with them. If it is a good one, we may be well disposed and will welcome feedback. If our history with the person was not all that good, we could be unwilling and uncomfortable to accept it. The mood of the person giving feedback at that time is also important. We can perceive this based on their tone of voice, gaze, posture and gestures. If we know or we sense that they are bent on criticizing us, we will have the feeling of being accused and may not accept the feedback but rather return it to the sender. If instead the person is benevolent, we can accept what they tell us in a more constructive way.

Before giving feedback, we need to make sure, in addition to the type of relationship we have with the receiver, the reason for which we intend to give it. The two main reasons are to confirm that their behaviour is appropriate and, therefore, encourage them to continue like this, possibly strengthening it, or to correct something, putting them back on track. Other reasons that, unfortunately, are often in place are to appear pleasant or to release our venom against someone. These two modes usually

---

[7] Helen Keller, *The Story of My Life* (New York: Doubleday, Page & Company, 1903).

occur in the presence of an insufficiently balanced interpersonal relationship. An example of the first is a phenomenon that is commonly seen when a parent wants to seem terribly interested in their little child's growth. The parent, in these cases, feels the need to comment on any action, however trivial, by saying 'bravo,' even if, for example, the child momentarily falls and, as expected, gets up again. The second phenomenon, the destructive outburst, happens when the person giving the feedback has some unfinished business. Maybe they say things like, 'How incompetent and stupid can you get.' The receiver hardly accepts such comments and their reaction tends to be, 'Did you look at yourself?'

We must also weigh the importance of the action for which to give positive feedback, that of reinforcement and encouragement. When given too often, or for trivial things, feedback loses its effectiveness as well as risks contributing to the narcissism and egocentrism of those who receive it. This is the sort of egocentrism that leads the person to think they are still the centre of the universe.

How to give feedback? This is not just about data and information, but it also has a relational dimension which contributes to the sense of pleasure and pride, increasing the quantity of dopamine circulating in the system. Dopamine contributes to the ability to learn and survive and the desire to seek it seems biologically preordained and inevitable.

To give reinforcing feedback, it is, therefore. necessary to say two things, one is what the person has done that is right and the other is the relational framework in which to package the message, for example, saying that we liked what they did. These two dimensions together can give rise to the following examples of feedback, 'I like how you dedicated yourself with focus and perseverance,' or 'I like how you lightened up that situation that risked degenerating into a conflict.'

To give balancing feedback, for example, referring to an action to be corrected, it is necessary, first of all, to discover and appreciate the intention, that is, to keep in mind that there is always a valid reason for which the person acted in a certain way and of which we may not be aware. The next step is to suggest or evoke how it would have been better to act and then conclude by encouraging the person to continue on the new identified track. An example, in a work context, after having ascertained the intention of the person would be to say, 'I understand that you wanted to save time and also wanted to feel independent and for this reason you neglected the reaction of your colleague, but how could you have achieved the agreed goal and at the same time fulfilled your personal priorities?' We can stimulate an answer by asking the person to remember examples from the past when they had already expressed the ability we are asking them to call upon. The approach is the same even when the context is non-business but family related.

It is particularly important, in the cases of balancing feedback, to make sure not to attack the identity of the person, but to refer only to the specific behaviour of the person. Since it is not always so easy to separate these two aspects, a useful technique, when there is the need to correct someone and there is the risk that the person will take it too personally, is to avoid too much direct eye contact. We can, for example, indicate with one hand the place where the behaviour to be improved took place, looking more at our own hand or where it is pointing than at the person.

On the part of those who receive balancing or corrective feedback, it is necessary to realize that the condition of being alive means that we can slip and get up again and that we can transform wounds into wisdom. We can learn from our mistakes, overcoming the infantile notions that success is a reflection of self-esteem. We can also stop seeking approval constantly. Mistakes allow us to unlearn and relearn, unlike navigation systems on cars that simply recalculate the path for us.

We can also learn from the example of Thomas Edison, the inventor of the incandescent light bulb, who, after a 1,000 attempts, said that he had found 999 responses to other questions. Or as one great artist said, every unsuccessful picture was just another opportunity to practise. So, any failure could mean that we are one step closer to the conclusion. We can continuously improve because we are not immobile statues that will only deteriorate over time. We would also like to avoid thinking that thought continuously repeated in space missions, that failure is not an option, because it is an approach that, when generalized to other situations, has the unpleasant smell of machismo.

Feedback can, sometimes, be one of the few valuable novelties in our day-to-day life, considering that, on average, we have 50 thousand thoughts a day, 95 per cent of which are the same as yesterday, with few variations. Of this 95 per cent, 80 per cent are said to be negative. Giving feedback could be a great rebalancing opportunity.

RESILIENCE

Resilience is a term that derives from Latin and means to bounce back. It refers to the ability of a material put under pressure to withstand a shock and regain its original state. Applied to the human sphere, we can speak of the ability to bounce back, to reacquire one's condition of fullness after a fall or an unfortunate event. It is the ability to react with the spirit of adaptation and with mental elasticity.

The great writer Maya Angelou, who died in 2014, is an excellent testimony of resilience. As a child, she went through many difficulties but never gave up. One of her most famous quotations is to be found in these words, so dense of meaning: 'You can shoot me with your words, you can cut me with your eyes, you can kill me with your hatred, but nevertheless, like dust, I will rise!'

Another example of resilience concerns the life of Nelson Mandela who, after 27 years in prison, came out in great shape, ready to become the president of South Africa. To lessen the weight of the years of his imprisonment during apartheid, he was inspired by the following poem written by the English poet William Ernest Henley.

It matters not how strait the gate,
How charged with punishments the scroll,
I am the master of my fate,
I am the captain of my soul.[8]

Even Helen Keller, a blind and deaf person, said she did not dwell too much on limitations and did not let herself be saddened by them. Sometimes, she wished she did not have them, but this was a vague desire, like a breeze blowing through flowers. She said that the wind had passed, and the flowers were happy.

All these people, like so many others, did not give up in the face of difficulties. For them too, their problems were caused by negative situations, but rather than stopping in the face of difficulties, they resolved to move forward. Had they stopped, they would have greatly risked succumbing and ending up in that condition of total defeat known as hopelessness, convinced that there would be no way out. Even worse, they could have considered themselves unable to find a solution, if there was one, thereby living a condition of impotence and helplessness. Such an attitude can bring a person to believe themselves to be inadequate and unworthy in an attempt to bounce back and recover in the face of adversity. This condition is called worthlessness.

What to do to be resilient and not give up immediately in the face of difficulty? A good way to start is to become aware and to accept that life is also made of important moments of negativity which, like the breeze that is blowing, will not last forever.

---

[8] William Ernest Henley, 'Invictus,' Poetry Foundation, https://www. poetryfoundation.org/poems/51642/invictus

As Joseph Campbell said, life is a great opera, but, sometimes, it hurts a lot. It may be useful to think that problems will not leave us until we have learned all they have to teach us. Sometimes, therefore, falling does certainly remind us that we are still human and that we are still alive. These considerations make us humbler and more sober thereby avoiding, as the Greeks would say, hubris, in other words, excessive arrogance and pride. This was, unfortunately, the attitude with which Prometheus challenged the deities in order to steal fire for humankind, only to fall ruinously, destined to suffer every day at the mercy of an eagle.

We need, from time to time, to welcome and experience this dark side offered by problems because it makes us more ready for the great experience of life. At the same time, we can ask ourselves if it is the negative element that is ruining us or if it is our choice to dwell too long on it. It is said, in fact, that problems have their charm, deceptive and, at the same time, seductive, as is the dark side of the force. But we don't need to make a nest inside them or stay in their grip and become a victim of the situation. The solution, even if not immediately visible, could be right there, at hand, for example, by opening the umbrella or putting on an overcoat when it rains.

It is said that problems will always exist, and the problem is not the problem itself but the way in which we see the problem. We see the world not as it is but according to the emotional state in which we are, in any given moment. It would, therefore, be useful to enable ourselves to escape from the stronghold of a problematic situation, to put ourselves in another emotional state, a more positive one, in which we can have access to many more resources and, therefore, many more useful choices, in order to ride the situation rather than being trampled by it.

The process of generating a more useful emotional state for facilitating resilience means beginning to reconnect with one of our parts, a part of great well-being, hidden right within us under the mountain of problems. The approach is to take refuge, and this will allow us to face the situation with a different attitude. And it reminds us that we are not worthless people. Believing that we are worthy and nurturing this feeling, on the other hand, motivates us to give our best even when we are under pressure.

A refuge is not an escape but could be considered a sort of internal exile, where we withdraw in those particular moments when we need to find some safety or when there is the need to restore ourselves. These are places that remain etched in our memory as experiences lived in the past, one of the most important being that of childhood, characterized by the care and the protection received from an adult, especially from our mother. And for those who do not have such vivid memories, the refuge could also be created by other experiences of sponsorship, for example, by anyone who offered us compassion, warmth, security, hope and happiness throughout our lives.

Recalling or, better still, reliving these experiences, especially managing to create a moment of stillness inside, perhaps, by means of a few deep breaths, serves to restore our organism back into a state of fullness. We will, thus, be better able to face the possible adversities of the moment, whether these are born in the external world or within our internal world. This technique of resensitization, widely tested also in the laboratory, can even be triggered subliminally with the use of words associated with emotional security, perhaps, by speaking them aloud. Some examples of such words are closeness, love, embrace, support. The pleasant emotions that they evoke will activate certain neurotransmitters including dopamine and opioids. These substances tend to favour the approach to solving problems rather than avoiding them. And every time we find a solution we will have more positive emotions, which will contribute even more to our capacity to be resilient.

Stopping for a moment in our place of internal exile, without wanting to return to the amniotic fluid of the womb, can be a panacea for our sense of self. As has happened to most of us as children, being looked after by someone who was important to us was something like medicine. These were moments that created an appropriate emotional attachment for us in which we saw the other as a safe haven or as the Dalai Lama says, someone in whom we could place our hopes. These were important experiences that contributed to our sense of self-worth. And seeing ourselves through the eyes of someone who loves us allows us to say, quoting the artist Winslow Homer, that everything is beautiful outside my home, inside my home and inside me.

Another equally important approach in being able to bounce back after a fall is flexibility and the ability to improvise. When a moment of adversity comes, it is useful to know how to use our own resources in an unusual way, imagining possibilities that others do not see, a kind of mental bricolage. We may ask ourselves if it is the adversity that is affecting us negatively or if it is our choice to stay in that condition for too long. It might also be useful to put ourselves in another's shoes, for example, a doctor, journalist, architect or any other professional, and ask ourselves, from the shoes of this person, to what extent we are seeing the situation in a distorted way and which would be a good way out. Maybe, we can also draw up a plan for our future development.

Always remembering to accept the problem with due respect, examining it to understand what it wants to teach us, without trivializing it, without being too optimistic and without trying to see only the positive side at all costs.

We will not take ourselves too seriously, we will not give too much importance to the ego, but we will take into account the fragility of human condition and of ours too. And we will remember, however, that with time, even negative situations will pass.

39

WHERE THERE IS A WILL THERE IS A WAY

When you have a why, you could bear any how.

—*Nietzsche*

Give me a place to stand and I shall move the world, said the well-known mathematician and physicist Archimedes. This is the reasoning on which is based the principle of the lever, a tool that can be used, for example, to facilitate lifting a weight. It is a reasoning that also applies to our everyday life when it comes to motivational leverage. Maybe we need to start a business, but being a little demotivated we need something that translates 'have to' into 'want to.' Once the motivation has been found, the difficulties will almost certainly be reduced and we will be able to perform more easily. In other words, 'have to' turns into 'want to' and this, in turn, allows us to find the way to carry out the activity in question.

We can see this phenomenon as early as at the start of our day. We do not always get up with great energy and enthusiasm. Sometimes, it is a physiological need that pushes us out of bed. There are other moments, for example, going on vacation or even taking a long and challenging journey to meet our loved one, when our will is so strong that we wake up very early and leap out of bed with great enthusiasm and motivation, ready to board the train or the plane that will take us to our destination.

In these cases, it is not just the place where we need to go or the person we will meet that motivates us, there is something beyond the goal, there is a reason of great importance that ignites a strong desire in us. This component that goes beyond the goal, why we perform certain actions, is called the meta-objective, and it concerns what is less tangible, less objective, more subjective and much more emotionally significant. It could also be one of the differences between human doers and human beings.

Going back to talking about the vacation, the place has its own importance, but what really motivates us is the why, that is, the benefit, the added value that the experience offers us. It could be the well-being that we will have, the warmth of friends we will meet again, the laziness we will enjoy or the activities that will give us new vigour. These constitute the meta-objective and when wanting is at these levels, there is such an abundance of energy that it reduces many difficulties.

The meta-objective is the part connected to the satisfaction of doing something that we believe has a return. It is the sort of fulfilment that will make us feel, in a sense, more complete, more of what we were before. Many will remember the sense of euphoria in the presence of a great success, or when we fell in love, how we felt we could touch the sky with a finger but, above all, we felt like another person, stronger, more balanced and, at the same time, more in harmony with the rest of the world. This is typically how one feels in the presence of the meta-objective that added value beyond the goal.

Sometimes, however, even the meta-objective can be blurred, especially if the expected results are not attained. A trip by car to reach a strongly desired place that lasts for hours due to endless traffic jams could play tricks on the emotions of the driver, making them forget their meta-objective, the reason for the goal and, consequently, the goal itself. Mother Teresa of

Calcutta, when she felt abandoned by God, entered a phase of disappointment in which she wondered if her mission, her meta-objective really had any sense.

As we can guess, even the most beautiful and noble meta-objective needs constant maintenance. This helps keep it always present and motivating. So, once we have established what our goal is, we can continue to refine it, making it more attractive. Something that is attractive stimulates the desire in us to get closer. In nature, for example, colours signal to insects on which plants to land for pollination. Or the display of their feathers on birds during the period of courtship serves to attract the mate. Similarly, we can build a beautiful image of our meta-objective, creating a mental image of it or even drawing it on paper as if it were a picture, abstract or straightforward or in whatever style appeals to us. Once the drawing is completed, we can pause a little to embellish it even further, perhaps, adding a touch of colour here and there, a source of light that makes it more luminous or even adding an object that we believe can complete the picture and make it more attractive.

Who is not so fond of drawing can use a phrase, a mantra to be repeated with awareness whenever they want. This practice, which comes from spiritual and gospel chants, creates a state in the person in which the non-conscious part is activated, the part that really guides and regulates our entire organism. Anyone can enter such a state, simply by repeating a single word dozens of times, focusing only on the word, without distractions, without thinking about the consequences and without letting themselves be distracted by thoughts that might intrude. This is a condition that is often characterized by a lightness of the mind in which our goals can shine, thanks to the brightness that the meta-objective acquires. We feel more eager and more ready to face challenges that previously seemed insurmountable.

Another way to increase our motivation is to be with people who are not only concerned about performing, but in turn have a meta-objective, preferably similar to ours, and by adopting one of these people as a model. Once we have identified the person, our unconscious, our non-rational part will tend to create a sort of emulation, that is, we will tend to do as our role model is doing.

Of course, this depends on the commitment we put into letting ourselves be inspired. It is the well-known Wimbledon effect which describes how the quality of the game, even of an amateur tennis player, tends to improve during the week of the tennis tournament, once the spectator has succeeded in identifying themselves with a champion and finds inspiration in him or her.

To understand why these techniques work, we need to remember that what we believe about ourselves or what we are made to believe conditions our way of thinking and, therefore, our actions. This is called the self-fulfilling prophecy, a phenomenon that has also been used in some teaching experiments. In one class, the teacher was instructed to use words that would reinforce the self-esteem of the students, while in another class, the teacher was instructed not to make any such comments but just to carry out the school program. The first group had much better results than the latter.

This is also the basis of the placebo effect that applies to drugs that are essentially made up of just water and sugar. The latest data show that when they are administered with conviction directly by the doctor, using appropriate verbal and non-verbal language, the placebo effect is so powerful that they produce results in up to 50 per cent of cases. This effect is reduced to 6 per cent when the same drug is administered by a nurse, probably because she is considered to be less authoritative than the doctor. The placebo effect, according to the Harvard researchers, also occurs in cases where the patient is informed that the drug is only a placebo. Even in these cases, the willingness, albeit induced by external sources, finds a way to translate into action.

Something similar happens in sport, when we ardently want something, when there is a very strong why, we succeed in overcoming limits that previously could have seemed unbeatable. An example concerns running the mile in four minutes, an enterprise deemed impossible before 1954, the year in which Roger Bannister created a new record. The surprising fact is that once the record had been beaten, this continued until a new limit was reached, a new barrier, a new conviction, a new limiting belief. What we believe and what we want to believe serves to harness energy in a direction, which is expressed in the capability and the power to reach our goals.

When willing something does not lead to the power of action, it could mean that some knowledge is lacking. If, for example, we do not know how to build a chair, all the wanting and willing in the world could serve very little. The will instead serves, in this case, to motivate us to go to carpentry school.

Sometimes, however, knowledge comes from unexpected sources. It is the example of the mother who succeeds in breastfeeding her adopted child, being convinced that this is her duty and wills it with great pleasure and enthusiasm.

40 OBJECTIVES

Obstacles are those things that arise when you take your eyes off the goal.

Setting a goal is an important factor in achieving results. It keeps us anchored on a path, minimizing the risk of deviating and wandering. Although deviations are sometimes very useful, first of all, because they serve to stimulate our creativity, and second, because they have been responsible for the evolution of the species, it is, however, important to follow an agreed objective, especially where other people are involved.

In the famous story by Lewis Carroll, when Alice, in Wonderland, asked the Cheshire cat which road to take, the obvious answer was that it depended on where she wanted to go. The conclusion of their dialogue was that if Alice did not know where she wanted to go, it did not really matter which road she took. This is not to say that one cannot get to one's destination without good route planning, after all, a broken clock shows the right time twice a day. But this is an event that does not depend on us and on which we have very little influence.

One of the factors that is considered essential for achieving a goal is its correct formulation, respecting certain requirements.

The first is that the objective be formulated in positive, affirmative language, towards a solution, what we want to achieve or improve rather than what we need to avoid. This is for two reasons, the first is the postulate that energy flows where attention goes. If a person says they do not want to be sick, poor, or any other negative condition, it is likely that the objective will be conditioned by the focus on discomfort and, therefore, energy could go into amplifying the negative situation. The person could be continually sucked right inside the condition they are trying to escape from. It is, therefore, necessary to ask which condition we wish to attain, aiming to express the goal in terms of achieving an optimal condition instead of coming out of a discomfort.

Another reason to formulate the goal in positive language is that our unconscious, non-rational part seems to be unable to compute negatives. When we say to a child, for example, not to touch something, their non-rational part will first build an image of having touched it and then erase it. It is a process that is rather challenging, even in adulthood, because some traces will usually be left in the mind of the image of the forbidden or undesired thing, and this will tend to attract our attention in that direction. The classic example is if someone tells us not to think of a pink elephant, internally the first response is precisely that of the pink elephant, and only through insistence and perseverance will we succeed in creating an image of a different colour. This is also one of the reasons why in education, whether in school or in sports, it is considered incorrect to give too much importance to errors because by highlighting them, they tend to repeat themselves.

The second requirement is that the objective be under our own responsibility. Wanting something to happen without our own commitment, without intervening to make the necessary corrections is more of a dream than a goal. It is like wanting it to stop raining and when it doesn't happen, we may take it out on someone. Or wishing that our colleague is nicer to us without doing our part to make the relationship more harmonious. Or wanting someone to love us without our making ourselves lovable. It is the desire, or worse, the expectation that the world changes according to our desires, a typical characteristic of self-centred people. It is also typical of the child who expects that the world will function as they wish, usually because there is someone, an almighty father, who will take care of all their needs and will make sure that everything will be adjusted, so that the world corresponds to their requests. Surely, some factors that are external to us can help determine a successful outcome, but without an intervention on our part, without using our own knowledge, the goal would remain only a pipe dream and often a perpetual complaint.

A third requirement is that the objective be contextualized. This means that the more important the objective, the more we need to establish, with precision, the boundaries within which we wish it to be fulfilled. If, for example, a person who is always or often aggressive aims to be milder, more accommodating and relational, this certainly will bring immense benefits in certain contexts, maybe with family or friends. But if they were to find themselves in the street, facing a possible robbery or having to face a thief in the house, the mild attitude in these contexts could be less indicated. Generally, in the face of any danger, when at risk is one's own survival or that of another person, the most useful attitude, inherited from reptiles, is to face the situation, attacking it, or to run away, both reactions that require a surge of adrenaline, that is, the opposite of an accommodating attitude. Of course, there is a third alternative, that of freezing, as animals sometimes do, feigning to be dead so that the predator will leave them in peace.

Any change that a person can produce will affect the entire system. According to the butterfly effect, moving our hand moves the surrounding air and this changes the overall balance. The more significant the movement, the more significant will be its effect on the system. When establishing a goal, it is necessary to take into account the length and breadth of the situation. The first concerns the long-term effects regarding the future, while the second concerns other people, who could be possibly involved. If the larger system, including its length and its breadth, is not able to accommodate the result, any attempt to change could meet obstacles that will make us take one step forward and three steps backwards.

This is, then, the fourth requirement, respect for ecology. And it also applies to us. If we are used to behave in a certain way, it means that we managed to find a functional niche in which we could obtain certain benefits. A person who shows a reaction of anger or arrogance towards others, surely manages, because of these attitudes, not to be dominated, not to be dragged into the vortex of certain situations and, most likely, manages not to lose their self-esteem.

Probably, this has become their usual, though not optimal, way of maintaining a just balance in those circumstances. Wanting to change this attitude could result in the person being more courteous, less impulsive, which surely are good ways of acting, but by doing so, they run the risk of not being recognized anymore and of losing their self-esteem, even if this was based on attitudes that were not exactly respectful. The same consideration applies to someone who suddenly becomes rich, because, if not evaluated from the point of view of ecology, they risk finding themselves unhappy because of the envy that could be generated among their acquaintances.

The fifth and final requirement is that the objective be of a proper dimension. This means, in particular, not wanting to eat the proverbial dinosaur in one bite. A trend, certainly favoured by consumerism and the speed with which the world moves, is that of wanting to get results quickly. Especially today, when just a slight pressure on the button of a remote control is sufficient to have an immediate change of scenery. We want to have everything and all at once. But at once is only a dream, which becomes an objective when we put a precise date to it. Knowing how to wait is an important quality, as it is for the farmer before seeing the fruits, or for a mother who must be patient for nine months while awaiting the birth of a child.

Proper chunking of an objective means breaking it up into parts that are more easily achievable such as defining the completion date and taking into account our availability of time. It is also necessary to take into account the availability of other people who will be involved. Successfully achieving each single stage contributes to providing extra motivation to take the next steps.

We can, however, take advantage of scientific discoveries and the technological means we have available to give us a hand to speed up the achievement. If, with all this, we are still not nearing the goal, it is necessary to verify again the accuracy of these five requirements, being able to respond to the inevitable setbacks in a timely manner.

And, perhaps, we must realize that life is what happens while we are busy planning or, maybe, we have forgotten that one sure way to make the gods laugh is to tell them that we are making plans.

ILLNESSES AND AILMENTS

Become mature enough to understand how the tragedies of life are included in its majesty.

—*Joseph Campbell*

Once upon a time, there was a beautiful tree that grew at the entrance of a village, and everyone who passed by would stop for some time to admire it. It was the pride of the village as it donated beauty to the landscape around. People even travelled long distances to appreciate its splendour. One day, however, it fell ill. But not the whole tree, exactly just one half of it. Looking at it, it appeared to be divided in two, the left side was sick and the right side was healthy. There were heated debates over its fate. Its presence, for some, disfigured the landscape and they wanted to cut it down, while others were still so fond of it that they remained unperturbed. After several meetings, the municipality, in an attempt to please everyone, decided to remove only the sick half, leaving the healthy half standing. What remained was no longer all that ugly. But as we can well imagine, it was so unbalanced that shortly after it fell down.

Regarding our health as well, when an inconvenience takes place, in the hurry to get rid of it our priority is usually to avoid dealing with the suffering part, as if it does not belong to us. And fortunately, pharmacological interventions do, sometimes, bring relief, but symptoms may return after a period of time, not to mention the unknown side effects of any chemical treatment that are only discovered with use. Without denying the validity

GRACEFUL LIVING

of the drug, we can also proceed in another way which could, sometimes, give more lasting results.

It is, first of all, necessary to reflect on whether the discomfort is connected to any difficulties that the person may be experiencing, of which they may not necessarily be aware. If, for example, they are not convinced to go on vacation to a certain place but, for some reason, did not get the chance to express their reluctance, it is not uncommon that they could get hurt a few days before departure, to the point of having to be hospitalized, thus, preventing them from leaving. This happens because the body, the tangible part, and the mind, the intangible part, are so interconnected that one influences the other. What happens in one of the parts manifests itself in the other. The person's reluctance to make a decision is reflected in a movement of the body, perhaps, the leg analogically refused to perform a certain action and the person stumbled, getting hurt.

In this case, we can also speak of a positive intention, a supposed benefit that is motivating the action and wanting to restore the body to a state of stability, security and happiness. For example, when someone has a fever, it is because some part of the body is reacting to an invasion of harmful agents which, if not stopped, could lead to disastrous consequences. A sore throat has a similar function due to defence mechanisms that protect the body. Sometimes, these mechanisms go haywire, activating themselves even in the presence of a reduced amount of stimuli, in other words, they trigger excessively. Examples are hay fever and other allergies.

The way we deal with a condition of illness is also conditioned by the awareness that, if ignored, it could degenerate into something worse, which could lead to more serious consequences, excessive suffering and, at worst, death. This is a consequence that nobody wants to contemplate before their time has come, a time which is difficult to predict, even though not impossible. The prospect of death brings several fears which, even if unfounded from a rational point of view, go on to further influence the condition of those who are suffering. Some of these fears are those of abandonment, loss of one's identity and being forgotten forever. This is the moment when some turn to religion which, according to some scholars, was born precisely to try to respond to certain fears and to manage the mystery of death. For others, the doctor is seen in a similar light, one who is able to alleviate suffering or, in extremis, to revive a dying person.

We want nothing to do with the so-called scary face of death, and we do all we can or, at least, we think we do all we can to avoid seeing its face. We tend to deny everything we believe is the contrary of good, we deny Satan, invoking the classic 'get thee behind me'. The rotten half of the tree is so difficult to accept that we forget the message of Shakespeare in his opus *As You Like It* that every toad, though ugly and venomous, wears a precious jewel on its head.

Accepting, instead, the message that is being offered can lead us to discover parts of ourselves to which we did not pay attention. In the field of health, we find that we were exaggerating in a certain area, for example, concerning work, food or sport, and that this led to fatigue and to a lowering of our immune system. Or we were conditioned by popular rumours that made us believe that, at a certain age, some diseases or ailments are inevitable. Maybe, we lived with the belief that the ailments that manifested themselves in parents at a certain age will manifest themselves in us too at, more or less, the same age. We are, thus, subjected to the concept that wanting to believe translates into reality but in a negative sense. This is no longer the placebo effect but the nocebo effect.

When ailments afflict us not only in the field of health, we worry, perhaps, excessively about how to get rid of them, neglecting what it means to regain a state of health. We worry more about cancelling the situation of hardship or the illness, rather than returning our system to a state of integrity, well-being and happiness. And the risk is that this way of communicating with ourselves does nothing but increase our worries, creating more wear and tear on our system and leaving less resources available for healing. And it is a further confirmation of the postulate that energy flows where attention goes.

First of all, we must accept that the part that hurts or is sick belongs to us, even if at first it seems to be a stranger, and we can then create a little more space in which it can transform. Usually, when we are ailing, our internal space becomes constricted. We are worried and, consequently, tense, and if we can identify where we feel the ailing part, we will almost certainly realize that it feels like there is a pressure, a weight or a knot inside. When instead, after a few breaths, we imagine we could let the space widen, the level of discomfort is lowered, like a liquid that is poured from a full container into a larger container, the container is no longer full and this translates into a lessening of the tension in our body. We will feel less distressed, a little more relaxed and we will be able to draw upon more resources to assist our recovery.

An important resource is compassion, understood as the reflection that there is a part of us that suffers and that this part does not deserve to continue suffering. With this in mind, we will tend more towards healing than repairing or treatment. Healing means inviting the body to work as it was designed to work, that is, in an integral way. The focus is no longer necessarily on eradicating the symptoms but on creating or recreating a balance, even if the ailment or illness should persist. It is important, in this approach, to formulate a health goal in positive language. For example, instead of saying that we do not want to have this illness or we want it to disappear, we could express the goal as wanting to have the possibility of managing our health to support the relationship between mind and body. This allows us to restore stability, security and happiness as it was before the ailment, when we were feeling good. With this approach, we avoid hating the sick parts as if they did not belong to us.

Finally, it should be noted that healing is not an isolated activity. Sometimes, we think we are separated from others, I am me and you are you, and we forget the interconnection that runs between all forms of life, whether human, animal or plant. When we realize that we are even made of the same matter as the earth, a whole new scenario opens up. We can feel part of a wider whole and we can entrust our healing to the collaboration of several elements. Even a simple caress, for example, given to a person or to an animal, can bring about a sense of greater well-being because, from a neuroscientific point of view, it activates certain hormones and neurotransmitters for our health and for our healing.

And let us remember that the very drugs we use are the fruit of the work of human beings that operate on substances that were all made in the great forge of the universe. Just like we were too.

42   LOVE AND HATE

Hatred, that uncomfortable feeling which is nothing but the twin of love.

Legend has it that Jason, in search of the Golden Fleece, the mythological cure against all evils, had to pass between rocks that, clashing erratically against each other, made the access dangerous to boats, often causing their shipwreck. Jason let a dove fly between the rocks which, with their unpredictable motion, managed to pinch only the dove's tail. From that moment on, the rocks remained still, and boats could easily sail through.

The passage between two contrasting sides, this meeting of opposites is a motive that is found in many traditions of universal wisdom. It refers to the dualities that contain, on the one hand, the illuminated side and, on the other, the shadow side. Some examples of such dualities are me and you, where the you is a non-I, life and death, good and bad, beautiful and ugly, fear and desire. They are also known as heretical opposites, in the sense that neither is right, but a good balance in any adventure, including that of normal daily life, means passing between dualities and polarities without attachment to one or to the other.

Another pair of opposites, which deserves our attention, is that of love and hate.

Usually, in the society in which we live, it is almost taboo to talk about hating a person. Such is the prerogative of the dwarf Grumpy, in the tale of *Snow White and the Seven Dwarves,* and he is the only one who is allowed to bask in this state. Perhaps, due to moralistic teachings, a declaration of hatred, often, generates in the so-called well-meaning people comments like, 'You're exaggerating,' 'You mustn't hate' and other similar expressions. For a parent, perhaps, one of the worst things to discover is their child telling their brother that they hate him. There is the fear, handed down through the millennia, and now, embedded in the collective unconscious that the feeling of hatred can degenerate into what happened with Cain and Abel.

We are witnessing, however, an increasing number of episodes of this kind, in which hatred manifests itself, unfortunately, in extreme gestures of destruction of human lives in the family as well as in society, in general. Some people attribute this to the ease with which weapons can be obtained, but it is more useful to think that we do not want to see the dark side inside us which, eventually, ends up possessing us. We thought we had buried hatred by not naming it, but as it is well known, a dog does not forget where it buried its bone, which manages to re-emerge in some of the least opportune moments and take hold of us. This is a phenomenon that is also seen in the world of social media, where the word 'haters' is part of the normal vocabulary and describes those who spread hatred in the network. Partly due to envy and other unresolved issues of which these people are not aware, they find themselves possessed by the impulse of hatred, with which they cannot do without.

There is a great difficulty, particularly in the Western world, to recognize and, therefore, deal with uncomfortable emotions. 'Don't cry,' is an exhortation that we often hear, not just to comfort those who cry, but because whoever says it is so distraught that they would like to put an end to what is bringing them discomfort, namely someone's crying. The reason is not only the inability to accept those who suffer but also because of various 'think positive' movements, which do not want to leave any space for our negative aspects and, therefore, end up refusing these parts. Get thee behind me Satan, again. Even the word 'problems' is not used anymore in some circles, some prefer to call them opportunities, whereas weaknesses become areas of improvement. But the most important problems are too complicated to describe with a simple rephrasing or reinterpretation of words.

If, on the one hand, we can appreciate the intention not to amplify and worsen the negative state by placing our attention beyond measure in that direction, on the other hand, we must realize that rampant goodwill does nothing but increase the inability to manage the so-called demons, in this case, that of hatred, a demon with which life inevitably presents itself. It is useful to recognize the shadow side, pausing for an appropriate length of time without getting trapped by these demons, without the negative aspect becoming our primary filter through which to interpret life.

Moreover, we can realize that each of these emotions, love and hatred, is the reverse side of the same coin. There is a popular saying that you only tease the one you love; meaning that according to how the coin falls, it manifests itself either as hatred or as love, certainly not as indifference. As in the legend of the clashing rocks, one cannot exist without the other. We can train ourselves to be receptive to both aspects of pairs of opposites, in the words of Tenzin Gyatso, the 14th Dalai Lama, who declared that no human emotion is foreign to him. This is just one of the reasons why he is always open to human suffering, it is not a facade but a sincere way of going through life.

When we find that we are capable of hating another human being, there is another discovery behind the corner, that is, the hatred we have towards a part of us. It is a part that may have disappointed us, made us feel inadequate. We know, particularly at an unconscious level, that this exists within us, but we do not know where it is and we do not want to look for its abode. As usual, it is easier to point our finger externally, to see the speck in our neighbour's eye but not the log in our own. And so, we feel authorized to commit acts of discrimination, to carry out hate campaigns against entire categories of people which can easily degenerate into genocide. If we had accepted that we, too, were able to hate, perhaps, we could have expressed this feeling in a more useful way, for example, hating the sin but not the sinner. We may have been able to dedicate ourselves to just causes in the attempt to bring more sanity to the world.

Love and hate must travel in concert like our two jaws. We will not succeed in nourishing ourselves if one of the two is missing, or if we should shut our mouth so tight that we cannot distinguish the two jaws. What is important is not to be attached to either one. But to let one touch the other. We can let these two aspects, with their wandering movement, like the waves of the sea that break on the shoreline, generate energy, a relationship that includes and transcends each of the two parts.

What word could describe this relational energy, which is larger than the sum of its parts? It is the vital energy, made up of opposites and the dynamic tensions that dance together like the notes of a symphony. In one moment, the movement is sweet, amabile, now it turns into something dramatic, in a more Wagnerian style. We never know what the next movement will be because we suspect there is a magician, inconspicuous and veiled with deception, always ready to disseminate hazards along our path. And we fall again. And right there, where we stumbled turns out to be the source of what we were looking for. Only when we descend into the depths of our being can we discover and recover the treasures of our life. And when we look back on life, as Schopenhauer said, it looks just like a disaster, one surprise after another. Only later do we realize that it was the plot of a great opera and rightly so. It could not have been otherwise because it was our journey, our life journey, that journey which is unique for every human being.

It would, therefore, be useful to ask ourselves what we can learn from hatred, yet another example of the ugly and venomous toad that conceals a precious jewel in its head. It could be that it wants to teach us how to have greater acceptance of the other person, or of our own aspects that we do not like. It could be that it is telling us to leave certain attachments behind, to bring a sense of humour and to realize that we can still grow. It could simply be that it is teaching us how to touch the situation with a hint of inner peace, as if we were sending a dove through the rocks. It could be that it is telling us that the more we surrender to the mystery of the universe and to its duality, without trying to dominate it, we will feel safer in its arms. It could be that it is inviting us to find the jewel inside, the light in the dark, knowing that the darker the night, the brighter the stars shine.

A practice that could train this sense of inner peace is to sit down comfortably and breathe rhythmically. We may remember, or even better relive, an experience in nature, immersed in its beauty, in front of a majestic sight, for example, a sunset, waterfall, mountain top, stormy or calm sea. These are moments when we are entranced and we go beyond the grip of the conflicting parts.

In everyday life, we can train ourselves to open up by listening to our favourite music, chatting with a friend, even about something not too deep, greeting someone we do not know or offering him or her a smile. These activities tend to generate certain chemical substances in our body, one of which is oxytocin, which serves to facilitate bonding with others, despite the subterranean and omnipresent hatred.

And so, we can choose not to live too long in its domain. When we nourish hatred, somehow, we hope that the other person will suffer because of its effects, but really, it is to ourselves that we do greater harm. The stronger the hatred, the more concentrated is the poison that we drink in the hope that it will always be the other person who dies.

43   THE LIFE OF A COUPLE

For one human being to love another, that is perhaps the most difficult of all our tasks, the ultimate, the last test and proof, the work for which all other work is but preparation.

—*R. M. Rilke.*

The life of a couple usually begins with falling in love. Of all that has been written about this phenomenon, the story of Tristan and Isolde is probably one of the most emblematic. Tristan fell in love with Isolde; thanks to a love potion which was not meant for him but which he drank, thinking it was wine. When he was faced with the fact that he had drunk his death sentence, he said he accepted that. Furthermore, with the prospect that he would be condemned to eternal torment in the fires of hell, considered, at that time, to be even more serious than death itself, he said that he accepted that too.

The nature of the love potion remains a mystery because falling in love often starts at an unconscious level. Even though from a biological point of view, one could say that two people get together to guarantee the propagation of the species, as happens in the animal world, from a sentimental point of view, it is not clear why people choose a mate. According to the tradition of the troubadours dating back to the 12th century, the eyes are the explorers for the heart, and it is the heart that sends the eyes to look for a pleasing image. When they find one, they offer it to the heart and if the heart is kind, love is born.

In the period of falling in love, it is all sunshine and puppy dogs and each member of the couple does their best to please the other. If they go out for an ice cream, they will probably both enjoy the same flavour, or one might even give up their favourite taste to nurture a sense of commonality. Differences tend to disappear, the two people want to share pleasure on a mental, sensual and physical level. The paradigm for falling in love is that in which, according to popular traditions, one goes out of one's head for the sake of other. For some, there is a sense of finding their other half so that they become complete in this unity.

According to popular tradition, this state could last up to seven years, when, finally, one realizes that the beloved is not only spirit and heart, but also has a part of the body that touches the ground, namely the feet, as highlighted in the painting 'The Ascension of Christ' by Salvador Dali. While before they were entranced by the sublime traits of the other, now they begin to put back their heads on their shoulders, those heads that they lost, perhaps even desperately. Some gestures that were a source of enchantment become a source of annoyance, the veneration ceases, the companion is no longer their muse, their inspiration but regains their status as a human being, full not only of merits, but also of defects. When they get angry, it is hard to recognize them; they no longer look like the same people they were when they first fell in love. Some details that might have been simply a source of curiosity, for example, how they squeezed the toothpaste tube, could now become a source of discomfort. This is the moment when blinds are lifted from their eyes, and what emerges from the legendary pond is so different from what had been imagined. It has the semblance of a frog.

For some, it is the end of the relationship; there is incompatibility, separation and divorce. For others, instead, it is the moment when falling out of love makes room to start loving. While falling in love was and is a feeling, love is more of a skill, it is the ability to look in the same direction and not only into the eyes of the other, as Saint-Exupery said. It is the time when life projects are born, oriented towards the future, going beyond immediate satisfaction.

And it is also the moment when the concept of respect takes on another meaning. In the phase of falling in love, respect was for the other person and meant taking into account their needs and desires, a sort of meeting halfway, each one giving up a part of their ego for the good of the other. In the phase called love, renunciation is no longer towards the other person but for the sake of the relationship.

The relationship is to be understood as a new energy that includes the two people and, at the same time, transcends them; in other words, an energy is referred to the whole which is greater than the sum of the individual parts. It means that choices are made based on a sense of us, a sense that goes beyond the individual egos. The sense of us is what gives life to the relationship, what the two people together can share and fulfil. For example, they can procreate and it is the merit of both. Each one gives their 100 per cent, it is not a question of fifty-fifty. They can be a model of connubial serenity for others, and it is not the merit of the individual parts, 50 per cent each, but a 100 per cent of the couple. This energy of the couple is what permeates every action, each doing their hundred per cent share, and this is what nourishes collaboration, respect, sensuality, in a word—love.

As change is inherent in life, love is also in continuous flow. People do not remain the same both physically and spiritually, and the ability to love is to evolve together with the other. Even the best marriages seem to include moments of forgiveness that are declared and, also, others not declared. It can be said that the couples who remain together in love are those who have renewed their vows at every significant period of transition of their life as a couple; for example, becoming parents, inserting their child into the school system, supporting them in their growth and finding an agreement in life's choices that are not necessarily shared by both at the start. Changes are also seen because of the child; as he/she becomes an adult and leaves the house, it creates an emptiness that the two parents are called to fill with their presence, renewing their sense of love for each other. It is a troubled period that risks exposing the couple, even if mature, to unforeseen stresses, the empty nest syndrome, when there is risk of separation despite having lived several years together. Other transitions concern the physical changes of each, such as menopause, becoming grandparents, entering the third age and the arrival of unexpected diseases that shows that every rose has its thorns.

Renewing the oath in the couple does not, necessarily, mean making a ceremony, inviting guests and investing large sums to entertain them—all aspects that may only be a facade. A deeper way is to recognize that there is still a common thread in the relationship with the person with whom we share the house, even if it is not the same as it was in the first years. This is a moment of great compassion, understood as wanting the good of the other, and of empathy, like feeling into the partner as if both were one, again a unit greater than the sum of the two parts. And it is also a moment of tenderness that can be witnessed seeing an elderly couple walking hand in hand in a nursing home. Another way to reinvigorate the relationship is to retrieve some real or imaginary photographs of the moment of falling in love, thus, allowing the aspects of the companion that were attractive to shine again in one's eyes.

Long-lived couples seem to find an automatic adjustment to the changes, thanks to their tested mutual adaptation. It is as if their life together was a kind of soup that remained sufficiently on the fire so that the flavours of each could blend, and this mixture manages to absorb the new changes whether small or large.

Welcoming this union means leaving the attachment to the ego early in the relationship. According to the renowned psychologist Erich Fromm, it is necessary to go from, 'I need you, so I love you,' to 'I love you, so I need you.' Although the sense of need for a person could seem romantic from the point of view of Hollywood, it is something that threatens to create attachment and addiction, squeezing the vitality out of a relationship and making it flat.

A short extract from a poem by Roy Croft summarizes the concept of love like this and perhaps it is this, after all, what love is all about.

I love you, not for what you are,
but for what I am when I am with you.
I love you for putting your hand into my heaped up heart,
And passing over all the foolish, weak things
you can't help dimly seeing there.
And for bringing out into the light all the beautiful belongings
That no one else had ever looked quite far enough to find.

The most mature need would, therefore, be that of being aware that to express love, we need someone who can receive it, value it and reciprocate it in such a way as to bring continuous renewal and vitality to the union with another human being.

In the words of the famous Beatles song of 1967, *All you need is love.*

44 THE HERO'S JOURNEY

Living is a form of not being sure, not knowing what next or how.
The moment you know how, you begin to die a little.

—Agnes De Mille

The hero's journey is a concept that draws its origins from the works of Joseph Campbell, later developed by Carl Jung. This theme, universally present, is the basis of the most beautiful adventure stories and the best films of this genre as well as is the leitmotif of the Homeric epic *Iliad*. It is a theme that recurs every time we talk about change, learning and, in general, when it comes to doing something unusual and leaving our comfort zone. It is a theme that inspires us to grow, to express more than what we are currently doing and, if understood well, transforming the world into a place that shines with joy for all.

The metaphor of the journey is always inviting us to go beyond the status quo and to overcome the inevitable obstacles and unforeseen events that we encounter in our journey, events that are increasingly frequent in today's VUCA world. In this anagram, the V stands for volatile, that is, the fixed points of yesterday do not remain as such for a long time because things change; the U stands for uncertain, that is, the roads are not like they used to be, a young man today may not even know what he will do when he grows up, because his future profession has not yet been invented; the C stands for complex, which means that more parts of the system are intertwined in every decision, thanks, also, to globalization and to a greater awareness of the environment in which we live and the A stands for ambiguous, which describes the condition in which truth is neither black nor white but can reside in both of these fields, that is, based on a sort of grey, hardly decipherable at first sight.

The hero is he or she who gets the trophy and brings it home. In common parlance, the hero achieves a goal that allows them to bring improvements to their life and into that of others. Mythologically speaking, the hero goes through a huge amount of challenges, performing valorous acts at a physical or a spiritual level, for the benefit of a community. In a sense, we are all heroes already from the moment of our birth. This in itself was a journey that was in no way trivial, even if it has been repeated for eons. We passed from one state to another in a very short amount of time. Conception is another heroic journey, since just one among the thousands of spermatozoa made it, that is, was fertilized.

The journey, even if the concept is well known, is unique for each individual. Surprises abound and they occur in forms that are not necessarily related to past experiences. Everything seems new, mysterious; no one knows where the journey will lead, because if we knew in advance, it would mean that the life we are living is not authentically ours. In actual fact, knowing which road to take to start the journey is, sometimes, the most challenging part. The hero, while taking cues from other heroes, will have to continually chart their own course to get to their destination.

The hero's journey can be divided into the following three main phases.

FIRST PHASE

The first phase is the call, which presents itself as a voice that is, usually, not well identified and is of uncertain origin. This call can come from within the person, who finds themselves, according to Dante, in a dark wood from which they want to get out. They realize that they are feeling uneasy, they feel that something is missing from their life, something has to be improved, for example, they must or want to abandon certain old habits. The call can also be solicited by external factors, for example, changes in the context in which the person works or lives. Perhaps, they find themselves playing a new role in the family, they have become a parent or have become a single parent. In an organization, they may have become the boss or may have changed their role. These are all experiences for which they would have had no specific training. The call could also be a consequence of natural disasters, or even artificial ones, they may find themselves catapulted into a new context due to insurrections or wars.

The first problem, especially when the call is born from within, is not being able to hear it or to decipher it. Maybe, we are too busy doing something else, maybe, we don't think that the bell tolls for us. We ignore signals that are still weak, for example, a slight pain that begins to make itself felt but to which we do not give much heed, perhaps, because we are too busy doing other things. Or the son who returns home in an altered state and we do not give enough importance to it, saying that it is nothing, it will pass, or the companion who overreacts to something we have said or done and we conclude, hastily, that they are nervous or tired and that they will get over it. These are signs that are calling us to take care of ourselves, our health, the health of relationships in the family and other interpersonal issues. Although deciphering them in the midst of the noise that has become cacophonous is not a simple thing, we know in our heart and soul that we will have to take care of them. We get up to do it, but it costs a lot; we are too comfortable in our comfort zone and we return to sit down, perhaps, even to sleep in that hypnagogic sleep where certain important things go unnoticed.

The call, however, becomes insistent and we know that the road to a new journey will be full of uncertainties. However, we are still reluctant and leaving the attachment to our old ways of understanding everyday life and relating to the world remains a difficulty. At the same time, our discomfort increases and so does the need to find a beginning to the journey, and continuing to look for it with courage, we surrender, at last, by will power or through sheer exhaustion, to the greater power and intelligence of the universe, which reveals itself to us in unexpected ways. 'Be bold,' said Goethe, 'and mighty forces will come to your aid,' in other words, the universe will dance around us and give us what we were looking for. This is the moment when the master arrives and, perceiving that we are almost ready, comes in the form of a mentor, coach, therapist or even a long lost friend to give us a hand, sometimes, even to give us the proverbial kick in the pants, so that we can identify the nature of the call and accept it.

SECOND PHASE

The second phase is the separation from our comfort zone and the consequent migration towards a goal, sometimes, not even clearly identified. The difficulty of leaving the old for the new persists, despite the fact that such experiences of separation are not new for us. We left, for example, adolescence to become adults, our life as a couple to accommodate the arrival of a child or we left our attachment to the eternal manifestation of youth to become more mature and, later, grandparents. The situation presents itself every time in a different guise and we return to being amateurs. Our human nature is strongly put to the test because we want to revisit our old patterns where the dots remain connected as they were before. Our doubts multiply and we are strongly tempted to retrace our steps, and since we are still at the beginning of the journey, we would like to say, 'To hell with the adventure.' But we realize that only by leaving the life we have, the life we are living, can we welcome the life that is waiting for us. And so, in grand career, we set off on our journey.

This is the phase of numerous transitions, which often seem to be nothing but going from one difficulty to another. If the hero is lucky, they find a journey that strengthens them, one that is full of obstacles, setbacks and challenges they will have to face. Sometimes, these can become threats for their safety, the so-called impetuous demons that frighten them and even seem to want to seize them, annihilate them or feed on them. And since they are all new experiences, they are not even sure they will be able to overcome them. But despite being a dilettante, they have past reference experiences of when they succeeded in facing similar, even though not identical, situations. Although they do not yet know how to overcome the present challenges, they know at least that they have survived the previous ones. The hero may stop for a moment to review the elements that contributed to success in the past situations and contemplate how to apply them to the present ones. But, in their condition as a dilettante, it will not be simple, and the most reasonable option would be to invoke a mentor or a coach who, traveling with them, sees the situation from a more detached point of view and would be in a better position to evoke or even suggest solutions more appropriate to the context.

This transition phase is one in which the hero needs greater resilience or the capacity to rise up again after the umpteenth fall, always keeping in mind the goal that attracts them to go on. And as in the best mythological tales and in the best adventure stories and films, the mentor or coach could also offer them a talisman, a symbolic instrument, the lightsabre in the *Star Wars* saga, or Merlin's invitation to find their inner strength to extract the sword from the rock.

The solutions, therefore, are not necessarily of a belligerent nature, aimed merely at destroying the proverbial dragon of St George, but could include getting to know these entities better, being incredibly curious to find out what lies behind their terrifying mask. The hero discovers that they saw these obstacles as threats because they were unprepared, frightened and, consequently, magnified them, making them appear even more serious and terrifying. They were lacking in certain tools, one of which was a sense of humour, a very powerful tool to neutralize the overwhelming power of demons in whatever form they present themselves and even, as is often necessary, to become an ally to them.

Thanks to these meetings, the hero will never cease to be amazed at how many resources lie within them yet to be activated. Once discovered, and with the necessary training, these resources become an incredible asset, which they will be able to use skilfully in other situations. This process is called learning.

The journey would not have been possible without the presence of mentors, ready to offer their wisdom when needed. In everyday life, this means encouraging us, sometimes, getting us to question ourselves, overturning our status quo and our limiting beliefs. Sometimes, the mentor may tell an anecdote which, at that moment, seems to have no connection with the situation, only to discover later, sometimes, even after many years, that the story was aimed at our unconscious, that non-rational part that already senses how we will need to move. And, sometimes, the mentor simply enlightens us by suggesting that we enjoy the journey, that we observe the flowers and smell their perfumes and, something very precious to keep in mind, not to be too attached to the achievement of the result.

The hero along the journey consolidates the relationship with mentors and guardians, even finding new ones and treasuring the learnings received from them. It is a support that will last a long time, even after the journey is over and even if the mentors are no longer physically present, they will become role models for the hero.

No one, said Joseph Campbell, can undertake this journey alone.

THIRD PHASE

The third phase is the achievement of the goal and the road back. Achievement means overcoming the last trials, usually, some of the hardest, since the trophy, although in sight, is guarded by even fiercer demons. It seemed to be all over and that these last steps would have been relatively easy, but the hero, like each and every one of us, needs to continually measure themselves against something that is slightly beyond their reach. The challenges, therefore, do not diminish and the hero will have to summon up other resources to make sure the journey is successful. But having covered a major part of the journey and being aware of having refined and developed many skills, the test could now be how flexible they are in applying them to the new contexts. The hero will never become an expert compared to something as big as life, but, at least, they will be a little less of a beginner.

Having passed the tests and obtained the trophy, which could be a metaphor for a higher level of understanding, awareness and mastery, the hero must return to the context they had left, so as to offer what they have learned. Were they to keep these boons for themselves, according to certain wisdom traditions, they would become acrid like smoke in a chimney that does not have a good draft. In some mythological traditions, those who keep what they have received for themselves die.

According to some schools of thought, especially those related to psychotherapy, the test of being healed, that is, to have overcome certain difficulties is to be able to pass on the fruits of our experience to other people. For the Alcoholics Anonymous, it is their 12th step to assist those in need. The generosity with which we give our gifts is an expression of gratitude with respect to the universe and will allow us to open ourselves further to receive other gifts that will come along our journey.

There are various ways of giving. It can be done with avarice, that is, giving what we no longer need or giving with our arm not completely extended for the fear that the recipient may take everything and leave us with nothing in hand. Another way of giving is the fraternal one in which we give without the expectation of receiving something back. Yet another, the most interesting for the hero is the regal way, with abundance, that is, giving one's best because we take delight in the well-being of others.

So, the hero returns home, but the demons are still at their heels, and when they least expect it, that is, almost at their doorstep, they encounter yet another extreme test, the one that could jeopardize their life. It almost seems as if it wants to test if the hero has become complacent, basking in the security of competence, feeling indifferent to the suffering of other sentient beings. At this point, they will have to sacrifice themselves again, that is, to leave the attachment to their certainties. Once this phase is over, which is a kind of resurrection or rebirth, their transformation can be considered well advanced.

The hero is, therefore, back at home, profoundly changed. Nothing will ever be the same again. They return to occupy their place in the ordinary world, but enriched with the elixir, the treasure and with the strength and richness of their learning from their journey, they will be ready to share their gifts with others.

The hero will also have to realize that even if they are full of gifts they are eagerly looking forward to share, others may not be ready to receive them and, in this case, they risk seeing their value quickly annulled. They will, therefore, have to manage how to offer them, avoiding, for example, flaunting their new abilities and, worse still, will have to avoid bragging about how many storms they had to weather. They will have to avoid searching for applause and praise, which are symptoms of the immature hero. They will then have to review how they are relating to others, whether they are creating the ideal conditions in which they can illuminate others without dazzling those who may still be in the dark. These are certainly aspects they will have learned on their journey.

According to the recursive nature of things, the end of a journey marks the beginning of a new one. What is the end for the caterpillar marks the beginning for the butterfly. Completing a cycle of studies at university, for example, means starting to work and giving back to the community what has been learned. We shall never cease to explore, the poet T. S. Eliot wrote, and the purpose of all the exploration will be to return to the point of departure and know it for the first time.

For the hero, therefore, having completed their task of sharing the gifts they received, there remains nothing but to embark on a new journey of dreams, explorations and discoveries.

LET THERE
BE DEMONS

You can't win, but there are alternatives to fighting.

—*Obi-Wan Kenobi*

According to the metaphor of the journey of the hero, each of us is called, sooner or later, to go on a journey. It is a journey that will lead to a fuller realization of ourselves and will contribute to the well-being of others. An important phase that can, sometimes, be like a scarecrow for the hero is meeting with the immense difficulties along the way up till the finishing line, difficulties that could risk the safety of those who venture towards any form of improvement.

Mythologically speaking, these obstacles are called demons, and in the Western world, in particular, they are not considered friendly. Indeed, as seen in some paintings, for example, in 'Saint George and the Dragon' by Paolo Uccello, they are to be beheaded. In actual fact, the hero is commonly perceived as the one who kills the demons.

Originally, however, the demon was a 'superhuman genius', also called a 'genius loci,' an intelligent spirit linked to a place, which accompanies and protects the place itself. In some cultures, it is believed that every person was born with a protective spirit that accompanied them throughout the entire arc of their life and could be recalled at critical moments. With the advent of Christianity, however, demons became evil, and, therefore, had to be eliminated. This thought is reflected in the tendency to hide our weak sides, our shadow side from the public. And so, we end up by not admitting, even to ourselves, that we have impulses which, if expressed, would not be tolerated.

This dark side, the shadow side tends to be sterilized, sanitized, especially in the Western world, blaming it on external factors and on the environment. We become, as Pink Floyd sang, comfortably numb. There are no more problems because we cannot tolerate that this concept exists inside us. Instead, there are only opportunities. This attitude is the politically correct escape which, although the intention is not to risk amplifying negativity in certain situations, ends up wanting to see everything through the lenses of Pollyanna, the naive optimist in the novel of the same name by Eleanor Porter.

The demon, this unknown and even mysterious part, scares us. But how would it be if we could welcome it, giving it space where it can breathe? How it would be if we allowed some of the world's dirt to enter us so that we do not live only in highly sterilized environments? How would it be if we were to put our hand in one of those garden hedges, home to a myriad of fearsome insects? What would it be like to play with mud, rediscovering that ancient pleasure of shaping it and feeling the contact, temperature and consistency of a substance that is also part of us? It is none other than an invitation to allow Dionysius, the one who lives underground, to return to being part of the mystery of life.

An allegory concerning the treatment of demons is the following. Imagine that in a garden there are edible fruit trees and other trees that produce poisonous fruit. The first reaction could be to cut down the poisonous trees. A second reaction is that of leaving them but fencing them so that those who walk around them will be safe. This is a decision based on compassion, both for the tree and for other human beings. But a third hypothesis is that of picking the fruit of the poisonous tree and turning it into substances beneficial to man, as is done in pharmacological practices.

The meaning of this is that we can take advantage of both day and night because we know that one cannot exist without the other. It is said that there would be no hero if there were no demons because these allow the hero to become stronger, more ready and resilient. The hero who knows the demons is better equipped to face the future. The hero who sees in the dark, where there are demons, are those who can also visit the places within themselves, their shadow side, where their own demons abide. It is said that when the eyes get used to seeing better in the dark, they come out with a broader view of life and of human nature, allowing us to understand it better in its vast complexity.

So, can the demon be put to good use? In India, they say that peacocks have such beautiful feathers because they eat a poison that they can transform into bright colours. In ancient cultures, different rituals are practised to honour the demons, to summon up a useful collaboration with them. In Bali, during the ceremonies to honour Barong, the good spirit, a portion of food is also left for his counterpart, Rangda. In Haiti, the festivities for Gede, in the voodoo tradition, serve to honour the dead. For Merlin, in the stories of King Arthur, it is necessary to stay in silence, rest in the arms of dragons, these beasts of enormous power that are found everywhere. And as the famous Austrian poet Rainer Maria Rilke said,

> How should we be able to forget those ancient myths that are at the beginning of all peoples, the myths about dragons that at the last moment turn into princesses; perhaps all the dragons of our lives are princesses who

are only waiting to see us once beautiful and brave. Perhaps everything terrible is in its deepest being something helpless that wants help from us.

One thing we learn when we face demons is that they are within us. They are not external entities but they are our inner energies, fears and desires that create tensions that are, sometimes, not very manageable. Ignoring them, without recognizing their existence, will result in their gaining strength and taking possession of us. Trying to eradicate them would amount to not recognizing parts of us, thus, risking to empty ourselves of a part of our vital lifeblood. As Joseph Campbell said, the demon is a consequence of attachment to one's ego. We are captured and chained in the dragon's cage and a therapist's job is to allow us to open the door of that cage and expand the field of our relationships.

Managing demons allows us to get up after falling, practising our resilience. Maya Angelou, like Helen Keller, are excellent examples of this skill and are just two of the many people who knew how to transform painful experiences into learning experiences. It is not simply a matter of getting up again as if nothing had happened, but to ask ourselves a few questions so that we can reflect and encourage an inner journey of exploration. The dialogue with these 'repressed' energies could start by asking:

- What is this genius trying to teach me?

- What aspect of me, which archetype is waiting to be activated?

- What is waiting to be born inside me?

- What new skill can I develop, and how?

- What conviction can I get rid of?

- What new choices are available to me now?

- Who can I become?

Again, to quote Rilke from his *Letters to a Young Poet*,

> We can learn not be frightened if a sadness rises up before us larger than any we have ever seen; if a restiveness, like light and cloud shadows, passes over our hands and over all we do. We must think that something is happening with us, that life has not forgotten us, that it holds us in its hand; it will not let us fall.[9]

One thing that is certain is that we cannot fall out of the universe. Therefore, let us not exclude discomfort, suffering and depression from our life. Only by meeting them and turning them into opportunities for growth can we achieve something beautiful, like gold that must be subjected to a high temperature to be transformed into ornaments. Or like bamboo that must bear being drilled so that it can be transformed into a flute that produces lovely melodies.

Dostoyevsky hoped only to be worthy of the suffering he had to endure. After all, we do not know how these states are working inside us and for us.

---

[9] Rainer Maria Rilke, *Letters to a Young Poet* (Mumbai: Yogi Impressions, 2003).

46

FROM STRAW INTO GOLD

Why be so enchanted with this reality when
a gold mine lies inside you.

—*Jalal ad-Din Rumi*

The fairy tale of Rumpelstiltskin, originally, Rumpelstilzchen by the Grimm brothers, tells of a dwarf who offers to spin gold from straw. This happened as a consequence of the vanity of a miller who declared to the king, who liked gold, that his daughter, besides being beautiful, was also able to perform this impossible task. The greedy, gluttonous king could not wait to have a wife that would have promised and guaranteed riches to his kingdom.

The miller's daughter, in exchange for the gold that would be spun from the straw, had to give the dwarf her necklace and, subsequently, her ring. But worse still, the third condition was that the girl should have to give up her first child that would be born out of her union with the king. The girl became queen and gave birth but had forgotten the promise, perhaps, because it had been made too hastily. But the dwarf had kept it well in mind and so he went to redeem what was due to him. The queen, as we can imagine, did not want to give the baby away and so started to cry. The dwarf offered her one last possibility, namely that if she could guess his name, she could keep her child. The story ends on a positive note as the queen, having sent some of her messengers around her lands, came back with the name of the dwarf.

Straw is something that has limited scope, its main use being for animal beds. So, straw could be a metaphor for fragments of information, also called notions, which are not yet organized, have not yet taken shape and are, therefore, still worthless. Gold, instead, represents something noble, a kind of divine illumination, a point of arrival. According to the tale, the ability to transform the base material into gold resides in all of us but may be hidden and kept in a corner of our psyche. The dwarf, Rumpelstiltskin, could be a metaphor for this creative part that we do not yet know.

To enable the transformation from the base material to something more valuable, it is necessary, above all, that we separate from some of our attachments. These are our certainties which, in the tale, refer to the frills, necklaces and rings that, usually, contribute towards the sense of one's identity. When our attention is perpetually turned towards appearances and towards the external world, it prevents us from taking a look at our inner world, at our own inner wealth and, consequently, at our sense of self. Sometimes, it seems as if we were willing to renounce, at first thought, some of our most precious things, those depicted in the tale by the first-born child, in exchange for fame and popularity, completely forgetting, as Dante suggested 'virtue and knowledge'.

But how do we abandon those certainties that, like some of the jewels we wear, remain so attached to us that they become a part of us and we even forget we are wearing them? Given, that once we are immersed, for example, in an environment of odours, we are no longer aware of what we are smelling, we must, somehow, get out of this situation to be able to appreciate it from a new point of view. This approach is the basis of any improvement, that is, to enrich one's own mental map with those of others.

We can proceed using the Johari window. This is a tool that allows us to reveal some of our areas that are under the radar. It can be facilitated by answering these four questions:

- What do I and also others know about me? For example, the colour of my jacket.

- What do I know about me but others do not know? For example, a wish of mine.

- What do others know about me but of which I am not aware? For example, how I smile.

- What do neither I nor others know about me? For example, when will I die.

This is a fun practise to do in company, and can be very revealing if done with appropriate lightness, not with the intention of hurting.

However, since attachment to the frills happens because, inside us, there could be a sense of emptiness, we can make use of external supports that will fill that void. As did the queen by sending her messengers around. Or as a parent does by relying on the support of a paediatrician and other essential figures for the growth of their child. We can send a request for support into the ether, knowing, as in the hero's journey, that guardians and mentors will arrive punctually to give us a hand.

Although we ourselves are the parents of our change from straw to gold, a few mentors can also give us a hand. Mentors can be those people who have already supported us in the past. They might be, for example, an old sage, a role model from real life or even from books, a friend we wanted to emulate and, perhaps, even surpass or anyone else who wished us success in an authentic way, not just as a social convention. It could be someone who believed in us, encouraged us, cheered us on, or someone to whom we have been supportive, someone in whom we generated a state of positivity. Once the mentors have been identified, we can create a silent space inside ourselves, through a few breaths, which will allow us to hear, or to imagine hearing that the mentors are telling us that we are still able to make the desired or requested improvements in our life.

With the support of mentors, we can, therefore, manage to give up some of those certainties that seem to keep us comfortable and happy in the so-called comfort zone, a zone which tends to diminish over time if not solicited with new stimuli. This is the area where the straw remains such, the area in which, although we continue to collect so many new concepts, we will not be able to transform them into gold, that is, to give a more cohesive and evolved form to the fragments, allowing us to make that leap towards a more complete understanding of the mystery in which we live.

Another important aspect in the story of Rumpelstiltskin is the discovery of his name. Until we can give a name to what is going on inside us, and even outside, everything could be a kind of great confusion, a condition in which we get lost or whose existence we ignore. For children, the fact of calling objects by their name makes their reality less fluctuating, thereby stabilizing it and is an important factor in their growth. For Helen Keller, the blind and deaf child, knowing that the substance she touched had a name opened up a new world to her which was, up until that moment, completely unknown and foreign. Finding the name by ourselves is not always easy; as in the story, the support of others is needed and, again, mentors can meet us in the guise of friends, colleagues and professionals of various kinds.

Even an adult needs a certain stability which derives, in part, from having certain reference points. As an example, let us imagine, for a moment, that we go to an unknown city where the streets have no names or numbers. We will have to make intense use of our other senses to orient ourselves, as sailors used to do. In the meantime, however, we may feel like being on the sea in a dense fog that seems to imprison us. In this situation, rediscovering our orientations can become an extremely arduous task, although not impossible. It is also the case of the tourist who visits a culture far removed from their own, for example, a Westerner who is on a street in Tokyo and struggles to see the difference between one person and another. So, they end up by saying that the Japanese all look alike. To an eye untrained to detect differences, everything that comes to us could seem equal to everything else, and this condition makes us stay in our cage of what is already known, preventing us from growing.

A fun practise that could also be done in company that allows us to get to know each other more deeply is to ask the question, 'Who are you?' followed five or six times by the question, 'Who else are you?'

Knowing how to give a name to what we feel, therefore, seems important. This becomes even more important when we are in the grip of an emotional state that we may consider not so useful. In these circumstances, one of the first things is to recognize in what state we are. Otherwise, it is like feeling exhausted but without recognizing that, maybe, we have a cold, headache or that something similar is coming.

The second thing is to know where the emotional state is located. As in physical disorders whose symptoms have a seat, we can also perceive the dwelling of our emotional states, for example, they may be more felt in the area of the heart, through the acceleration of the heartbeat, or in the belly, through sensations of knots, weights, vices or in other parts of the body. Identifying the location of these symptoms makes them less imprecise, allowing us to proceed with an intervention. We can exploit the mind–body connection to imagine, for example, that we can expel them, through exhalation or that we can even extract them from our body, as if they were like a thorn in a finger.

We will be relieved, ready to continue our journey towards a further transformation of straw into gold, without having to give up that most precious part of ourselves, our inner child, our identity.

47   SELF-AWARENESS

Who knows others is wise, who knows himself is enlightened.

—*Lao Tzu*

Sometimes, it seems, paraphrasing James Joyce, that we live a little distant from ourselves. The speed with which things change, especially in our consumer society of disposables, is such that we do not even find a shred of time to be with ourselves. We are constantly bombarded by novelties, the latest model of technology, without which we are led to believe that we cannot survive. Television channels are in the order of thousands, we cannot live with only one, and so, some of us have acquired the taste of zapping from one channel to another in the constant search for new stimuli, because in the absence of these, we fear we will be forced to look inward and may end up finding a world too foreign and unknown.

Even as early as at school age, the pace of activity, sometimes, seems unbelievable. Many children are taken by parents from school and rushed off to do, sometimes, more than one sports activity before finding themselves again, literally or metaphorically, that is, returning home. In the world of work, a similar situation repeats itself, the arc of the day is long, the things to do are many and are all urgent and people are always in a hurry. Workplaces look like as if they are full of predators from which people are on the run. Many feel the tyranny of time when, in reality, it could be that the predator is the one that resides within us and has become like that because we feel so fragmented and bewildered that we hardly know who we are.

Despite all this, we meet ourselves several times along the journey of life, though in different guises and in different contexts. Often, this happens because we find ourselves repeating the same mistakes, in some of our daily choices. A significant example is that of people who leave one romantic relationship and start a new one, only to find themselves with the same identical problems that compromised the previous one. For some, the new girlfriend not only temperamentally resembles the previous one, but may even physically look like her. It really seems that we learn little from history and from our past experiences, it seems that, like Sisyphus, we are doomed to push the boulder towards the top of a mountain just to see it roll back to the base each time.

We can remedy this condition by starting to inhabit our body and our senses some more. Starting with breathing, and with each breath, we can think that oxygen is in love with us and does not want to leave us. We can picture how our body expands inside with each in breath and how, when we exhale, our body contracts as if to embrace us internally. We then allow our eyes to open to what surrounds us and to appreciate it. If we look out of the window of our house or the office, with a relaxed look, and continue doing so for a few more seconds, it is very likely that we will notice something we had not seen before. Maybe a colour or a shape because every leaf of a tree has a hue and a shape that is different from the others. We will be more present in our eyes. If we look at a wall, we will notice that it is not completely uniform but, here too, there are several irregularities. Even if we find nothing, we can simply let ourselves be captured by the beauty of the landscape we are observing or some aspect of it. And soon, we will find ourselves feeling more aware of our presence, of the presence of a life flowing within us and, at the same time, we will realize that we are part of the mystery that presents itself daily in front of our new eyes.

The practice of observation is also useful when we walk on the street and see so-called marginalized people. By extending our attention respectfully, we will be surprised to note how many aspects of beauty reside in them, also, like the diamond in the coal, the pearl in the oyster. Even the toothless old hag with a hooked nose reveals her beautiful appearance and this, too, is a new way of pausing to perceive what we had previously ignored. It is a way, according to Rilke, to go into ourselves and see how deep the place is from which our life flows.

The auditory canal can also bring similar results. By listening to a piece of music, we can imagine the instrument from which the music is emitted and how the player is holding it, how they are using it, stroking it or employing more force. We will be so much more present and aware; it will be like living inside our listening organs. Paying attention, also, to the pauses that are between the notes, we will surely find ourselves feeling that our awareness is expanding, to include more parts of us, like the artist who dips the brush into their soul and paints this experience on the canvas.

Even touch can help us get closer to ourselves, giving us a more complete sense of how we relate to things. Rubbing or stroking pieces of cloth of different textures slowly, maybe closing our eyes, we can not only appreciate the finer external differences, but perceive how these make us feel. Of course, we can also caress ourselves, massaging various parts of our body and experience the feelings of well-being that we derive from doing so. This is not a passive massage, like a masseur acting on the massaged, but it is a case of paying particular attention to the point of contact of the massage and to the awareness of how we are experiencing the internal sensations.

Movement is another way of finding ourselves and living more in touch with ourselves. While we walk, we can be aware of how we place our feet on the ground, first the heel then the tip, how we use our arms, eyes and ears and how our body interfaces with the environment. And if we perform the movements in slow motion, we will also be present in our muscles and in our joints.

Not to mention the well-known raisin meditation, that is, before eating it, to look at it, touch it, smell it, put it in our mouth without chewing, feel its consistency and, only then, biting it and listening to the noise it makes while chewing it. Finally, we can feel the taste as it descends into our throat. It is a practice that allows us to be more aware of ourselves, to be no longer so distant from our being.

We can also extend our awareness to places far away from us, as Martin Luther King used to do at breakfast. Coffee was poured into his cup by a South American, tea by a Chinese and the cocoa by an African. And we can visualize the hands of those who have cultivated the wheat for our toast and the other things that are part of the meal. Before finishing, we will feel connected not only with ourselves, but with more than half of the world. And it is a nice way to realize that we are a significant part of a whole, a part that matters because everyone is interconnected and is helping to keep the system alive.

But what happens most frequently, as Saint Augustine said, is that people travel to be amazed by the mountains, seas, rivers and stars and they pass by themselves without wondering. We see it every time a tourist decides to take a trip not so much to find themselves but to accompany their camera. Italo Calvino said that people do not travel to enjoy the 7 or 77 wonders of a place, but to listen to the answers that the place gives to their questions, answers that come when, in their inner silence, the person becomes aware of a life that flows within himself and of a connection with the world outside.

And here is a beautiful poem by Derek Walcott, the poet who was awarded the Nobel prize for literature in 1992.

The time will come when, with elation,
you will greet yourself arriving
at your own door, in your own mirror,
and each will smile at the other's welcome,

and say, sit here. Eat.
You will love again the stranger who was your self.
Give wine. Give bread. Give back your heart
to itself, to the stranger who has loved you
all your life, whom you ignored
for another, who knows you by heart.
Take down the love letters from the bookshelf,

the photographs, the desperate notes,
peel your own image from the mirror.
Sit. Feast on your life. [10]

It is a gentle, yet touching invitation to keep body, mind, soul and spirit engaged in this vital dance that is called life.

Where would we be without it?

---

[10] Derek Walcott, 'Love After Love,' in *Collected Poems, 1948–1984* (New York: Farrar, Straus and Giroux, 1987).

FORGIVENESS

If you want to fly, you have to abandon all that weighs you down.

Two monks are walking and, at a certain point, come to a stream. There is also a girl waiting to cross. The elder monk picks her up and takes her into his arms to carry her to the other side of the stream. He then deposits her so that she can resume her journey. The two monks continue in silence but the younger is evidently upset. After a while, he plucks up the courage to ask the other monk for an explanation for his gesture, given that they had taken vows that they would never be in such close contact with the other sex. The answer was immediate. The monk admitted that he had picked up the girl but had promptly left her once they crossed the stream. Then, he added that it was the other monk who was still carrying her with him.

This is a good explanation of the concept of forgiveness, one of the most complicated issues to manage. When asked to forgive someone, it seems that the request is to condone the action of the other. This may derive from certain attitudes of dubious origin, for example, to turn the other cheek, or to forget the wrongdoing, but such expressions have fallen a little into disuse.

A term that has become more commonplace today is to move on but, in the end, it looks like the same old wine in new bottles. The attitude of turning a new leaf too quickly is not very useful. When the Native Americans wanted to stop fighting, the custom was to bury an axe. But, as in the world of dogs, nobody forgets where they buried the axe or the bone.

We have the experience of having tried to forget, to leave the past behind, only to see it resurface when an event, a look or a phrase said in a certain way, immediately brings back to our mind unpleasant moments that led us to condemn the other person. The old wound has not healed, it is still wide open.

There is, naturally, a part of us that suffers when we think we have been wronged. Maybe, it is an exaggerated sense of virtuosity that leads us to a thirst for justice, when it really is a thirst for revenge. The resentment that weighs on us is due to the fact that not only did we feel offended, but also trampled by the wrongdoing, so much so that if we do not react to the situation and in a hurry, we are afraid of being annihilated. These are situations in which we continue brooding and dwelling on the past and we thereby allow the memory to continue to invade us. And the more we lash out against the other, the more our resentment grows. The more we scratch the mosquito bite, the more annoyed we feel. It is like continuing to drink poison in the hope that the other dies.

This is the moment of forgiveness. As the word itself says, it is a gift, but the interesting thing is that it is a gift we give to ourselves. We give something that allows us to lighten the burden that we are carrying, in order to face the situation with more calmness and balance. We need to re-establish a more intimate contact with ourselves, which we had lost by giving our full attention only to the wound. And the wound kept getting bigger due to the phenomenon that energy flows where attention goes.

Giving something to ourselves means regaining our awareness, becoming aware that we are still intact and that the world still loves us. We can offer the balm of our breath by being silent for a few moments and still love ourselves despite the pain.

In this way, we shift our attention to our well-being, and the result is that we leave the girl once we have crossed the river. Thus, we will feel stronger, which does not mean to annihilate the other person, that person who we think has offended us, but if anything, we will have the strength and the presence not to feed the part in us that is suffering and to let it go in peace. Meanwhile, we continue to deepen our awareness in order to make us more intact, less frayed. The result is that our relationship changes both with the wrongdoing and with those who have wronged us.

Changing the relationship does not mean ignoring the crime or even our consideration of it. We condemn the sin but not the sinner. We realize that hurt people hurt other people and that everyone acts according to a positive intention, clearly not perceiving the broader picture of the situation and, thus, creating damage in some parts of the system. To understand better what is the positive intention, we can think that the other person also has a history of difficulties and challenges to overcome, and that the way they interpret the world may not seem right to us but for them it is the best choice available. If we stop to think, we will realize that we, too, do the same. No one is perfect, no one is exempt from this myopia, simply because it is impossible to consider all the possible consequences of an action. Clearly, there are those who are more myopic than others and risk creating greater damage.

There is a beautiful story that one day Paul Watzlawick, an illustrious expert on human communication, was holding a congress with participants from all over the world. Of course, in a situation of the kind, with a lecturer of that calibre, it is assumed that everything he says would have been taken as the gospel truth. But for one person in the audience, it wasn't like that and he got up and said he didn't agree with what he had heard so far. Watzlawick remained silent for a moment, as if to honour the person's positive intention and then replied that if he had been in that person's shoes, he probably would have said the same thing.

We learn that to forgive is not to forget, rather we need to remember the wrongdoing and, if anything, act so that it does not happen again. If we do not remember, we risk repeating destructive actions, something that happens so often in the world. If we do not remember, we will not know what we are forgiving and the forgiveness risks being null.

It might be useful to sever a relationship with someone who committed something that we deem negative towards the benefit of humankind. The essential thing is to cancel the debt that we believe the other owes us. When instead we maintain the debt, we are the ones who hurt ourselves, while the other probably couldn't care less.

Gandhi said that the weak will never know how to forgive, it is an attribute of the strong. A great example of forgiveness is that of Mandela who, once released from prison, greeted his jailers in such an unexpected way, given the 27 years spent in prison. Mandela explained that if he had shown the reaction that would have been considered normal, that is being closed, angry and full of resentment towards those people, this would have meant that he was still in prison, in their prison. It would have been yet another weight that he would have had to bear and that would have prevented him from resuming his journey. The Dalai Lama is also an excellent example of forgiveness as he does not hold any grudge against the Chinese, despite their actions of unheard violence in Tibet. He even calls them his friends, and he is very sorry to the point of being moved if he sees a Chinese suffer.

The Amish people, a community of people who faithfully follow the religious principles of Christianity, had to contend with a massacre of 10 of their pupils in the state of Pennsylvania in 2006. What happened after was totally unexpected. The elders of the Amish community, despite their pain, did not blame the killer, did not point their finger at him. Instead, they went to see his family to bring some comfort to their pain. When it appears difficult to be compassionate with a criminal, it can be easier to be so with his mother, she is the one who almost certainly is stricken to know that her child behaved so terribly. The Amish, while condemning the violent act, avoided carrying a grudge that could explode in equally violent acts on their part.

Another example of forgiveness in action is what happened in Darfur. After the atrocious genocides, where many people saw their family members killed, the perpetrators of these massacres had been called to talk with the families of their victims, negotiating how they could make up for the wrongs they had inflicted. From these meetings, very useful approaches to forgiveness emerged, such as acquitting one's own debt to society and alleviating the burden of one's hurts. Hurt people, it is said, hurt others.

Forgiveness can, therefore, be considered as a gift that a person gives to themselves in the first place and, consequently, also, to the society.

49   HOW IT ENDS

Today is the first of the last days of our lives.

One thing is certain: every day that passes is a day that will never come back. Another thing that is certain is that we will not come out alive from this mysterious chaos called life. If, on the one hand, these seem to be sad considerations, on the other hand, they are an encouragement to live every single moment fully. Precisely because it is assumed that we will no longer pass this way again, at least, not in our current form.

Benjamin Franklin, one of the founding fathers of the United States, said that every morning when he woke up, the first thing he did was to go through the obituary column. If he did not see his name, then he could get out of bed. Vignettes of the kind with which we try to paint the face of death serve to lighten its load, which has been heavily weighed down by those religious traditions that depict paradise as an idyllic place, in contrast to the punishment of roasting for eternity in the fires of hell.

But death should not be something to be considered so serious, so foreign to life, given that it is part of our existence. As the day exists, so does the night. As birth exists, so does death. If this were not the case, this planet would not be able to contain all sentient beings. Steve Jobs called death the greatest invention of all time because it clears up the old to make way for the new. Honouring life also means honouring death.

According to a Buddhist thought, the measure of our spiritual development is determined by the way in which we face death.

The best is with joy, the second best is without fear and the third is with no regrets. We can, therefore, aim to give the best of ourselves, with generosity, and be at the service of humanity, allowing us to reveal the beauty and goodness that lies within each of us.

Many think that this is the best way to find oneself again. It would be a nice message to share with children, at an early age, since the things we learn as children remain etched in us even at a very advanced age.

If our intention along the course of life was to leave the world a little better than how we found it, and if we think we have fulfilled at least part of what was our life calling, what life wanted from us, then we will not have wasted our time. And when our body no longer works as it should, we can welcome death.

Even with loved ones whom we don't want to lose, we can learn to let go of attachments yet again and give them permission to leave when their moment arrives.

The well-known Indian philosopher and poet Rabindranath Tagore, in his collection of poems entitled *Gitanjali* offers this gem, reminding us to be grateful for whatever comes our way:

> On the day when death will knock at your door what will you give to him?

> Oh, I will set before my guest the full vessel of my life—I will never let him go with empty hands.

> All the sweet vintage of all my autumn days and summer nights, all the earnings and gleanings of my busy life will I place before him at the close of my days when death will knock at my door.

I know that the day will come when my sight of this world will be lost forever, and life will take its leave in silence, drawing the last curtain over my eyes.

Yet stars will watch at night, and morning rise as before, and hours heave like sea waves casting up pleasures and pains.

When I think of this end of my moments, the barrier of the moments breaks and I see by the light of death this world with its careless treasures. Rare is its lowliest seat, rare is its meanest of lives.

Things that I longed for in vain and things that I got— let them pass. Let me but truly possess the things that I ever spurned and overlooked.

I have got my leave. Bid me farewell, my brothers! I bow to you all and take my departure.

Here, I give back the keys to my house—and give up all claims. I only ask for last kind words from you.

We were neighbors for long, but I received more than I could give. Now the day has dawned and the lamp that lit my dark corner is out. A summons has come and I am ready for my journey.

At this time of parting, wish me good luck, my friends! The sky is flushed with the dawn and my path lies beautiful.

Ask not what I have with me to take there. I start on my journey with empty hands and an expectant heart.

I shall put on my wedding garland. Mine is not the red-brown dress of the traveler, and though there are dangers on the way I have no fear in my mind.

The evening star will come out when my voyage is done and the plaintive notes of the twilight melodies will be struck from the highway of the gods.

When I go from hence let this be my parting word, that what I have seen is unsurpassable.

I have tasted of the hidden honey of this lotus that expands on the ocean of light, and so I'm blessed—let this be my parting word.

In this playhouse of infinite forms I have had my play and here have I caught sight of what is formless.

My whole body and my limbs have thrilled with the touch that is beyond touch; and if the end comes here, let it come—let this be my parting word.[11]

This sobering and moving poem also reminds us to abstain from being too attached to any role in which we find ourselves, whether that be in our private or professional life. It teaches us to go with the flow of life, not trying to stop it by holding on too strongly at any point, or by pushing against the river. And it hints that we can appreciate any and all moments, including those related to suffering.

After all, isn't life, as well as its shadow and counterpart, death, a great learning experience?

---

[11] Rabindranath Tagore, *Gitanjali* (Kolkata: Rupa, 2002).

50   ONE LAST THING

I want to sing like the birds sing, not worrying about who hears or what they think.

—Jalal ad-Din Rumi

Following the line of thought of the well-known theologian and Trappist monk Thomas Merton, the book ends here but the search goes on. Even when the bells have finished playing, the sound continues to come out from those who listened to them. The scent is still carried by the breeze that continues to blow into the soul of each of us.

Life is a mystery to be lived and appreciated, said Kierkegaard. Although we are committed to doing and undoing, meticulously planning to achieve goals, we have no certainty where all this will lead us. The only certainty is that, one day or another, we will die, we do not know when and how, but we know it will happen. Even if this is certain, it seems we have ample power to choose how to get there. Mother Teresa made sure that everyone who came to visit her could go away in a better state, accompanied by kindness in her eyes, face and smile. Maya Angelou suggested being a rainbow in other people's clouds. The poet Alberto Rios encouraged us to be a river that gives its journey to another river.

Perhaps, all this is pointing us in a direction, a compassionate participation in the mystery of life. Living with a sense of constant gratitude to the universe that has been so generous as to host us and to the life that has been given to us. Not least, offering up ourselves generously regarding what we would like to leave for the future generations. Sometimes, we will not be able to do good for another person, but the sole intention, for example, to give alms to a beggar, according to the philosopher Gurdjieff, will unleash a series of events whose culmination will be that the person will receive what we wanted to give them. The universe, said Gurdjieff, is so interconnected that someone else will stop by to complete what we had in mind.

In any case, we will continue to ask ourselves what this life wants from us and, consequently, what will be our gift, and if we are really paying our debt, in a sense, the rent for our stay on this earth.

We would like to contribute to alleviate excessive suffering and, concerning those inevitable things, for example, disappointments, diseases, failures, we can appreciate that these too are part of the great design of life. Sometimes, the world might seem like a terrible place, but we can trust that these moments are forerunners of wonders to come. We can, therefore, rejoice even in these moments knowing that joy is the union of beauty and ugliness, and that one cannot exist without the other. In doing so, our inner harmony will also be reflected in the external world.

Living in harmony means leaving certain attachments; one, in particular, is the attachment to power over other sentient beings and also over nature, an attachment that is often reflected in pride, exploitation and indifference to life. We would also like to leave the attachment which is the mother of all attachments— the attachment to oneself. We would like to break down the consequent rigidities, those that are manifested in the ways in which we treat not only others, but also ourselves. We would like to be able to appreciate that everyone, including animals, is on their journey of becoming in a world full of enchantment, which is not some kind of magic but simply a way to enjoy every moment by experiencing it in a completely present way.

We would like to live in a world where we feel alive, without trying to show ourselves as infallible, but instead we can inhabit a world in which we can fall, fail and take advantage of feedback to get back up again. We would like to risk doing things not knowing if they will work but knowing only that they are important and essential things to do. These are the things that will contribute to the life of the future generations.

We can live life in all its moments with the knowledge that we are not the centre of the universe but we belong to something immensely greater than ourselves. We can live every moment with the awareness that our every action can contribute to the good of the environment in which we live, and the fruits will not necessarily be seen in our lifetime but will be one of our main reasons for existing. We can follow the example of Victor Frankl, a prisoner in the concentration camp who saw his closest relatives die, but nevertheless, remained determined to make sense of his life. He also noted that the people who had lost all hope, those for whom the future had ceased to exist, that is, to have any meaning, were those that were taken away first among the random choices for the gas chamber. Frankl continued to nurture his dream of offering his gift to the rest of the world, and when he was released, he created the school of logotherapy, based precisely on discovering the meaning of existence. This is a concept that is found in the term 'eudemonia,' that is, happiness that is not simply hedonistic, in itself, but is the most enduring one because it is achieved by creating something for the benefit of humanity.

Gandhi suggested living as if every day was the last day of life and Carlos Castaneda reminds us that death is our greatest adviser. Although these tips may seem bizarre, they are showing us a way, that of always living with the end in sight. It is a very useful teaching also for children. We can imagine what a world would be like if, already, at an early age, we were all oriented towards a collective good. And if we work every day in that direction, so that when our final moment comes, our swan song, we can rest knowing that we have played all the music that was inside us. We can say, with the famous poet Mary Oliver, that we will end up not simply having visited this world but to have experienced it in its beauty.

And what is beauty? It is something that is absolutely superfluous, as far as the functionality of things is concerned. If we take a tool, for example, even a simple kitchen knife or piece of cutlery, what matters is its ability to cut food. Some findings, however, along the banks of the Thames, dating back 500 thousand years ago, although resembling knives, had a disproportionately large handle compared to the blade. Being so impractical, it is suggested that these tools were used in a kind of ritualistic context. It is probable, or even possible, that they were not only intended to cut meat or food, but they were part of something less material but more spiritual. From this reflection, the poet Robinson Jeffers defined beauty as that which is divinely superfluous. The suggestion is, therefore, to do all that is possible in order to live life in beauty, trusting that every day the mystery reveals itself. And when it's all over, maybe, the time will come when we will actually meet ourselves, our divine part, that part which was ingeniously hidden throughout the whole arc of our lives. And for such an important meeting, don't we want to present ourselves in beauty?

We can repeat the ancient Navajo chant, which refers to the pollen path, a substance that was indispensable for survival in their agricultural society.

> *In beauty may I walk*
> *All day long may I walk*
> *Through the returning seasons may I walk*
> *With beauty before me may I walk*
> *With beauty behind me may I walk*
> *With beauty above me may I walk*
> *With beauty all around me may I walk*

Finally, we can take inspiration from the Australian aborigines who remind us that we are all visitors in this time and space and that we are just passing through. Our task is to observe, learn, grow and love. And then we return home.

And it all ends, does it not, in such a hurry, like the glow of a flash of lightning in the sky, like a torrent that runs down a steep mountain? Is it not true that what the caterpillar calls an end, the rest of the world calls a butterfly?

Is not true that the whole journey of life is nothing but a preparation to become again a non-person?

EPILOGUE

What will happen now? Every moment is an unrepeatable miracle, and tomorrow is forever.

When St Augustine said that we pass by ourselves without wondering, perhaps, he was alluding to perseverance. We realize that we will never understand the mystery that we are and in which we live. However, this does not exclude us from persisting to decipher it, opening ourselves, according to Rilke, to all that is extraordinary and eternal, letting ourselves be conquered by these things.

We will always be ready to ask another question and yet another and, maybe, one day we will be granted some answers. But only to the extent that we can abandon excessively falling in love with ourselves and our opinions and theories and thereby sever our attachment to dogmas, preconceptions and certainty.

It is a continuous search in which we will be serious amateurs.

An anecdote in the Sufi tradition tells that one day a pupil went to visit a sage and asked him, 'Great sage, I have to ask you a very important question, the answer to which we all want. What is the secret to a life lived well?'

The wise man thought for a moment and then replied, 'The secret of living well is to make the right decisions.'

'I understand,' said the pupil, 'But how do I know what the right decisions are?'

'That's the fruit of experience,' replied the sage.

'Yes, but how can I cultivate the experience?' the student asked.

'By making the wrong decisions,' said the sage.

Every mistake we make, and we will continue making them, every fall, is nothing but another opportunity to learn and grow. And by continuing to explore, perhaps we will come to discover amidst all the uncertainties, in the midst of the confusion and chaos, that we are perfect in our imperfection.

May we cherish ourselves and continue to travel in beauty.

AFTERWORD

This is a book of hope and wisdom. I have known Arthur Sackrule and his dear family for many years, ever since his son attended the Montessori school that I founded in Castellanza, Italy. I liked his discreet and gentle elegance and this book of his was a pleasant surprise for me. I found thoughts both new and deep-rooted in it as well as universally shared knowledge, some of which gave birth to *Quaderno Montessori* created with Arthur and other friends with the aim of guiding other parents to reflect patiently, as we tried to do, on the challenges that children were continuously playing out. About 40 years have passed since then, the world has changed so quickly (and not only because of COVID-19), yet there are still a lot of age-old things to save.

I have read and reread Arthur's book. Some themes that have particularly struck me are: The *king* and the *queen*, for example, symbols of yin and yang, who guide our species, where *demons* and dragons force us into continuous wars, whereas positive forces would indicate ways of *listening* to the other. I recognize the practical Buddhism in the chapter on 'Empathy and Compassion' or in the pages on 'Diversity' that pervades and keeps the natural world alive, a world where most of us humans would prefer uniformity and everything equal. Consoling is the chapter on 'The Life of a Couple,' today too often short; ties that immediately unravel because of the lack of mutual patience and to the bewilderment of the children. On the contrary, the beauty of lasting couples, indeed long-lived, as Arthur calls them, who overcoming the boredom of habits, resist finding new common interests and keeping alive the pact that allowed them to become that vital nucleus which we call the family. How? Here are the three phases suggested in this book, and so well analysed: above all, a form of 'Resilience,' a word still largely uncommon in the daily practice of the majority, a feeling that is the opposite of rigidity of prejudices and of actions, but instead a continuous movement towards others and at the same time listening to ourselves.

'Mirror Neurons,' admirably described here, struck me immensely, remembering how about 30 years ago I learned about them and this allowed me to understand better the meaning of the admiring gaze of very small children towards their parents. Hurriedly defined as imitation, to me—observing—it seemed rather a mirroring of adults, in general, an inspiration to invent something else, a phenomenon that is also found in us 'grown-ups,' every time we meet new emotions, new masters ...

I'll stop here. There is too much to say. A book that knows how to masterfully link the old and the new, forgotten concepts are resurrected here in very modern terms without ever assuming the tone of a sermon.

Thank you Arthur for this necklace of 50 pearls, each one more precious than the other.

—Grazia Honegger Fresco
One of the principle Montessori educators with over 60 years' experience, author of over 20 books, one of the last students of Maria Montessori, founder of the Castellanza Montessori School, Italy, and Honorary President of the Montessori Rome Birth Centre.
Sadly, Grazia passed away just a couple of weeks after writing this. Aged 91, she died peacefully in her sleep.

ABOUT THE AUTHOR

Arthur A. Sackrule was born in Trinidad in 1948. He graduated in philosophy from the University of Cambridge, England, in the days when the presence of greats like Bertrand Russell and Ludwig Wittgenstein was still felt. He specialized in logic, thereby uniting two worlds—the humanistic and the mathematical–scientific. He was later drawn towards the field of neurolinguistic programming (NLP) and, subsequently, graduated from the NLP University in California as a certified trainer in NLP.

His background draws upon diverse schools of thought, which include the approaches of Maria Montessori and Rudolf Steiner; the psychodrama school of Jacob Moreno; the approach towards autonomy, responsibility and awareness of Caleb Gattegno; the psycho-synthesis approach of Roberto Assagioli; not to mention the eclectic and ecological approach of Gregory Bateson. His work is also based on the latest discoveries in neuroscience.

Arthur's main interests are within the great wisdom and mystic traditions both from the East and the West, which he weaves into intricate patterns of great beauty and appeal. His main focus is that of unravelling and enabling others to unravel the puzzles and mysteries of life, whether personal or professional, as they present themselves in their most beautiful as well as most challenging aspects.

Arthur has over 30 years of holistic experience as a trainer and coach in the educational, business and therapeutic fields, to which he brings his vast expertise and care. His personal mission is to facilitate the inner harmony that allows every human being to participate fully and move with confidence in the great daily drama in which we are all called to participate.

As a trainer, he is a charismatic person who, in addition to facilitating learning and change, inspires others to evolve. He has the gift of being able to intersperse gems of inspiration in his training sessions to illuminate others to find their own path towards excellence. In the role of business executive coach and life coach, his compassion and humility allow him to free up the person's resources so that they can achieve their goals more efficiently and more effectively. He is a role model for others to walk their talk.

He works both with individuals and with well-known local and international companies, especially at board levels.

Arthur considers himself an eternal student of human nature, and never tires of refining and updating his approach towards his work and life. He enjoys walking in nature, which he regards as an extraordinary learning experience and which gives him a deep sense of belonging with the universe.

Arthur founded Educational Services in 1986 to offer the most exquisite form of training.

He has been living in Italy since 1970.

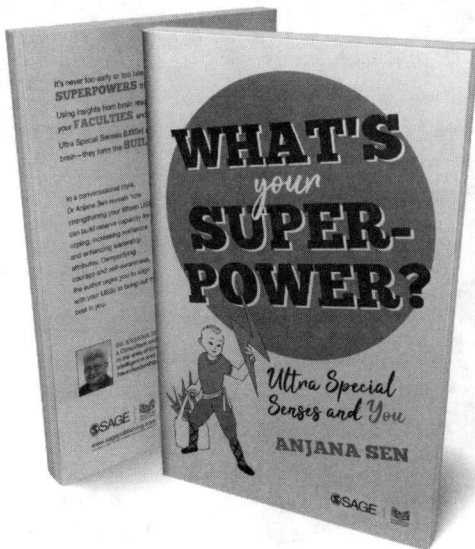